COURT TESTIMONY IN MENTAL HEALTH

ABOUT THE AUTHOR

Doctor Gerald H. Vandenberg is a clinical and forensic psychologist who has been in private practice in the Kansas City area for more than twenty-five years. His extensive forensic experience includes work with the courts and police. Doctor Vandenberg received his doctorate from the University of Kansas in 1966 and interned at Kansas University Medical Center. He is licensed in both Kansas and Missouri and is an American Board of Professional Psychology Diplomate in Forensic Psychology. He is a fellow of the American Academy of Forensic Psychology and a member of the American Psychological Association, the American Association of Marriage and Family Therapists, the Kansas Psychological Association, and various other state and local professional societies.

COURT TESTIMONY IN MENTAL HEALTH

A Guide for Mental Health Professionals and Attorneys

By

GERALD H. VANDENBERG, PH.D.

CHARLES C THOMAS • PUBLISHER
Springfield • Illinois • U.S.A.

Published and Distributed Throughout the World by

CHARLES C THOMAS • PUBLISHER
2600 South First Street
Springfield, Illinois 62794-9265

ISBN 0-398-05825-3

Library of Congress Catalog Card Number: 92-31403

With THOMAS BOOKS *careful attention is given to all details of manufacturing and design. It is the Publisher's desire to present books that are satisfactory as to their physical qualities and artistic possibilities and appropriate for their particular use.* THOMAS BOOKS *will be true to those laws of quality that assure a good name and good will.*

Printed in the United States of America
SC-R-3

Library of Congress Cataloging-in-Publication Data

Vandenberg, Gerald H.
Court testimony in mental health : a guide for mental health professionals and attorneys / by Gerald H. Vandenberg.
p. cm.
Includes bibliographical references and index.
ISBN 0-398-05825-3
1. Psychology, Forensic. 2. Evidence, Expert—United States. 3. Mental health laws—United States. I. Title.
KF8965.V36 1992
347.73′67—dc20
[347.30767] 92-31403
CIP

To my wife, Sue, without whose encouragement and support this book may have remained only an idea.

PREFACE

Mental health experts are increasingly called on to aid the courts and attorneys in a range of cases wherein their expertise can help to reach more just dispositions. This book is by no means intended to be an exhaustive review of an extraordinarily complex function but an introduction to the fascinating and stimulating field of forensic mental health.

This book is also written in hope of bridging the gap that lies too often between the mental health professional and officer of the court. Even seasoned professionals can regard each other if not with suspicion, then without full understanding, of the contributions each can make. However, each can learn from the other. It is hoped that this book will promote that process.

The author is deeply indebted to a number of people who have helped significantly in bringing this book to fruition. Donald Tiffany, Ph.D., reviewed the manuscript from the perspective of an experienced forensic psychologist and offered many helpful insights.

Particular thanks are due to Thad E. Nugent, Esq., who examined the manuscript with the seasoned and critical eye of an attorney well familiar with the use of mental health experts in the legal system.

The author is especially grateful to Susan Lindsay, who edited and polished the manuscript. Her craftsmanship and professionalism were of incalculable aid in completing this project.

The author also thanks Jeanne Harmon, who patiently typed and retyped early drafts of the manuscript.

Finally, the author thanks the many colleagues, particularly associates I. J. Barrish, Ph.D., and Harriett Barrish, Ph.D., and the supervisees, attorneys, and judges who offered inspiration and encouragement every step of the way.

G.H.V.

CONTENTS

Section IV—After the Evaluation

Section V—Other Considerations

COURT TESTIMONY IN MENTAL HEALTH

Section I
PREPARING TO SERVE THE COURT

Chapter 1

THE FIELD OF FORENSIC PSYCHOLOGY

Our judicial system is founded on the belief that individuals are accountable for their actions. However, the courts have also long held that many factors influence one's actions—the need, for example, to defend oneself. And so, individual accountability, while simple in principle, is not always simple in fact. Accountability is further complicated when the factors that influence one's actions are psychological ones and not so easy for the lay person to observe. Consider, for example, the plea of "not guilty by reason of self defense." That plea is relatively easy to maintain if witnesses or evidence attest that one's life is in immediate danger. However, "not guilty by reason of insanity" is rarely clear-cut. This example illustrates the conflict over two fundamental issues that has marked the history of mental health testimony. First, what is the relationship between "mental health" and responsibility for one's actions? Second, who may testify about another's mental health, and what may that expert say in court?

Early Descriptions of *Mens Rea*

Early Judeo-Christian writings address the first issue. They allude to the belief that various aberrations of personality may affect one's responsibility (Hermann, 1983). Children, for example, have been held to a lower standard of accountability than adults, as are adults with the mentalities of children, "madmen," "lunatics," and others deemed to have impaired mental capacities, however primitive the labels applied to them. Such forgivings suggest that there are degrees of subjective culpability for a crime, called *mens rea,* or, literally, "guilty mind."

In the 1700's, one gauge of these degrees was the "wild beast test." This test, first documented in England, held that individuals could be judged insane—and not responsible for their actions—if witnesses vowed that the accused didn't know what they were doing any more than "infants, brutes, or wild beasts" would (Melton et al., 1987).

The M'Naghten Rule

In 1843, a man by the name of M'Naghten tried to assassinate British Prime Minister Robert Peel but killed Peel's secretary instead (Melton et al., 1987). M'Naghten was acquitted on the basis of insanity, and his case formed a precedent still used in a number of states. The M'Naghten rule holds that people are not criminally responsible if, because of mental disease or defect, they do not know the nature and quality of their acts. The rule further holds individuals not responsible if they know the nature and quality of their acts but do not know that what they are doing is wrong.

Interpreted strictly, the M'Naghten rule is a cognitive test of mental state at the time a crime is committed, and elaborations of it, such as the "irresistable impulse" test, are discussed later in this chapter and in Chapter 6. Furthermore, the M'Naghten rule is quite narrow and does not address a defendant's ability to *control* his or her behavior. It recognizes only knowledge—or lack thereof.

Durham, and a Step Backward

In 1954, Durham vs. U. S. rejected M'Naghten in the federal courts. Indeed, the courts seem to have partly overreacted to the narrowness of M'Naghten by setting a far more liberal standard, that of the "product rule." Durham held that individuals were judged not responsible for their crimes if their actions were simply "the products of mental disease or defect." Unfortunately, the "product rule" was so broad and ill-defined that it beclouded issues instead of illuminating them; it set forth no criteria for defining what mental disease or defect characterized *mens rea.* Many criminals have personality disorders, especially antisocial disorders. Are these disorders mental diseases? If so, then ironically, habitual criminal behavior could be its own defense.

As a result of Durham, the second source of conflict surfaced, controversy about the testimony that experts may give. Many abuses followed when mental health experts made conclusions, often claiming some kind of "diagnosis" of "mental disease" simply by stating their opinions and not citing the bases for them. In 1923, the so-called "Frye test" (Frye vs. U. S., 1923) had defined expertise generally as making a conclusion from a scientific principle with sufficient general acceptance in its particular field. Thirty years later, however, courts more often saw experts "concluding" that a person suffered from mental disease or defect because that was the expert's "opinion." Such circular reasoning did little to establish to the courts' satisfaction that opinions are based on standards of practice or generally accepted knowledge within one's field of expertise. Furthermore, the expert sometimes trespassed on the domain of the "finder of fact," the judge or jury, by making conclusions of law in the name of science.

McDonald, and the Notion of Control

An attempt at clarity came with McDonald vs. U. S. (1962), in which the court defined mental diseases or defects as conditions of the mind which "affect mental or emotional processes and substantially impair behavior controls." However, while the decision did extend the narrow cognitive scope of M'Naghten to address one's ability to inhibit impulses, it did not clearly define the law's view of mental disease or defect. That was to come in 1972 with U. S. vs. Brawner.

Brawner, American Law Institute's Recommendations, and the Role of the Expert Witness

Brawner overturned the Durham decision and adopted the American Law Institute's recommendations for determining *mens rea.* The ALI test maintains that a defendant, by virtue of mental disease or defect, may lack the "substantial capacity to appreciate" the wrongness of his or her acts or is "unable to conform behavior to the requirements of law." "Appreciate" broadens the "knowledge" required by M'Naghten, and the "volition prong," which came to be known as the "irresistible impulse" test—the ability to conform one's behavior to the requirements of law—acknowledges the importance of control. Moreover, the ALI recommendations specifically exclude defenses of antisocial (then called "psychopathic") personality. Since then, conditions of "voluntary insanity," for example, drunkenness and substance abuse, have also come to be commonly excluded, although they may be used in some states to support defenses of "diminished capacity." This relatively new option to the insanity defense claims partial impairment in contrast to the all-or-nothing plea of insanity.

Just as important as defining criteria for responsibility, Brawner described the role of the expert mental health witness. The decision asked the expert not to conclude culpability but to describe the defendant's mental state within the bounds of the ALI criteria. Thus, mental health professionals can testify to the defendant's ability to distinguish right from wrong, the ability to contain impulses, or the general mental state at the time of a crime, but assigning responsibility is the job of the court. Testifying that a defendant is "insane," for example, is just beyond the province of the psychiatrist or psychologist.

Who Are the Experts?

As for who may testify about another's mental health, psychiatrists and medical doctors were the first to lend their services as experts to the courts. Psychiatrists (first called "alienists") have held the high ground on the witness stand for years. Psychologists are relative newcomers, not surprising when one considers that the entire profession of psychology is itself relatively new. In fact, the roots of modern applied psychology are in the twentieth century.

Not until 1962, then, in Jenkins vs. U. S., did the United States Court of Appeals hold that the lack of a medical degree was not a criterion sufficient to disqualify a psychologist from testifying as an expert. Rather, the qualifying criterion was whether the nature and extent of the psychologist's knowledge and the opinions derived from it could aid the "trier of fact" in the search for "truth." Whether the expert's opinions can add to the issues before the courts over and above the knowledge of the lay person is, indeed, the *sine qua non* for admitting expert testimony.

Although the role of mental health professionals as expert witnesses is still sometimes an uneasy one, psychiatrists, psychologists, and social workers are increasingly called upon by the courts to assist in the search for "truth," and their role as experts has expanded over the years. The mental health professional now testifies in a wide range of matters brought before the court. They are summarized below and discussed in detail in the chapters that follow.

Custody Evaluations: In these, among the most difficult and draining of cases, the mental health professional is often left to seek out the least destructive option in spite of the law's attempts to serve "the best interests of the child." Moreover, a mental health professional's custody recommendation *per se* often adds little to the long-range outlook for those immersed in the dispute, and solutions to the all-too-common acrimony between principals do not come easily. The most effective custody evaluations make reasonable recommendations to restore or improve stability and relationships in the child's world—and, one hopes, in the parents' world as well.

Criminal Responsibility Examinations: Mental health professionals are asked to determine a defendant's mental state at the time he or she committed a crime so that the court can judge whether the defendant was insane or suffered "diminished capacity," a lesser degree of culpability. The insanity defense, always quite rare, has become even more unpopular since John Hinkley's acquittal under it after his attempted assassination of President Reagan. Today, we hear more often of a defendant's impaired ability to form the intent to commit a crime that requires intent (murder, for example, as opposed to involuntary manslaughter which involves criminal negligence). By speaking of degrees, diminished capacity skirts the guilty/not guilty dichotomy which the insanity defense tends to impose and constitutes a partial defense to criminal responsibility.

Personal Injury Cases: Mental health experts may be called on to assess the degree of "mental or emotional trauma" from an accident or injury judged to be the "proximal," or immediate, cause of the trauma. They may also be asked to shed light on the extent of disability and the patient's prognosis in cases of head injury, "traumatic neurosis," adjustment to the loss of limbs or sight, and so on. In such cases, the neuropsychological evaluation may not only describe the injury itself but also address the individual's capabilities and losses, losses' effects on adjustment and future achievement, and expected rate of improvement.

Competency Hearings: There are two types of competency issues. Civil competency describes the individual's ability to manage his or her affairs. A civil competency hearing generally takes place in Probate Court at the determination of guardianship. Criminal competency describes the individual's ability to stand trial. Criteria for determining criminal competency include whether individuals are able to understand the charges against them and whether they can participate adequately in their own defense.

Commitment Hearings: A person's potential danger to him or herself or to society determines whether he or she should be committed to an institution. In emergencies, the courts can commit individuals for brief periods to assess these "dangers"; thereafter, full dispositional hearings take place.

Presentence Evaluations: After a defendant is found guilty but before he or she is sentenced, the court or an attorney may ask a mental health professional to submit information about the defendant, including personality type, motivation, potential treatment, and prognosis, to aid the court in appropriate sentencing.

Adjudications of Juveniles: Mental health professionals are called on to provide opinions that aid in deciding whether individuals should be tried as adults or juveniles. Specific criteria govern this choice, and some, like judging the "heinousness" of the crime in the eyes of the law or the prior record of the child, are beyond the scope of expert mental health testimony.

In all of these cases, the mental health professional as expert witness is a contributor, not a determiner, and psychological variables simply constitute pieces of a larger puzzle. Furthermore, the mental health professional assists by providing clear, sound, and relevant information in his or her role as an independent expert, not advocate. The chapters that follow discuss these general roles and responsibilities further. They also apply them in detail to the civil and criminal actions in which expert mental health testimony is called.

Other Aspects of Forensic Mental Health

This book addresses the mental health professional as an expert witness in the courts, but the role of the psychiatrist, psychologist, or social worker in the legal system is far broader. In fact, many forensic psychologists and psychiatrists have little to do with the court system at all. Rather, they serve other functions.

Police departments, for example, increasingly call on psychologists and psychiatrists to aid them in a variety of ways. Because the role of the policeman is highly visible, stressful, and potentially dangerous, mental health experts are often asked to assist in screening and hiring police recruits. They use various data—interviews, psychometric tests, research, and so on—to help achieve a successful match between applicant and assignment. One need only recall cases of alleged police brutality, especially when captured on videotape for public view, to appreciate the importance of this role.

The expert's role with police, however, does not end with personnel selection. Mental health professionals are also called on to help train police officers in handling emotionally loaded situations, notably domestic relations disputes—among the most dangerous situations officers face—and hostage negotiations. Mental health professionals also help police officers learn to cope with stress. While one might think that crises are the primary cause of stress, that is generally not the case. Most stress derives from more mundane matters, including the public's disdain for law enforcement officers, bureaucracy, rules, and regulations within the department, pressures within the family from relatives worried about danger, and long and erratic hours—all conditions leading to police "burn out" and an extremely high divorce rate.

Mental health experts may also consult to police departments in criminal investigations, although this is a rarer role. Some psychologists and psychiatrists are trained in techniques that contribute to the FBI's criminal "profiling," now called "crime scene analysis." The FBI's behavioral science unit has compiled characteristics and correlates of criminal behavior derived from extensive study, including repeated interviews, of various types of major criminals. Crime scene analysis applies these compilations to help identify and apprehend criminals. Mental health professionals may also use the so-called "psychological autopsy" (Schniedman, 1976), a determination of a person's mental state prior to death, to help determine whether the person committed suicide or was murdered. Similar techniques, now referred to as "psychological reconstruction," may be employed, for example, to assess an individual's state of mind when a will or other document is contested.

Mental health professionals function in the correction system by diagnosing and treating prison inmates. Psychologists' expertise in research techniques can be put to use in institutional settings, as Groth's and Birnbaum's (1970, 1978) study of sex offenders demonstrates. The research studied offenders said to be primarily fixated on children as sex objects versus those who preferred their age mates but sometimes regressed under stress to victimize children.

Psychologists and others are sometimes called to help in jury selection, and some psychologists specialize in this service. While research findings on the efficacy of their efforts are mixed, mental health professionals are nevertheless sometimes asked to help pick jury members thought more likely to favor a particular defendant's case. The techniques they employ include profiling, polling or survey methods, and evaluating potential jurors during *voir dire* or with questionnaires.

Mental health professionals without specific expertise in forensics work in the legal system as well. For example, researchers may be called to compile comprehensive, "state of the art" findings on particular issues such as the so-called Battered Spouse syndrome, the validity of eye witness testimony, or the effectiveness of polygraphs.

The Future of Forensic Psychology

The role of the mental health professional in the legal system is one of increasing responsibility and importance. Many believe that the aspect of that role which this book treats, expert testimony, also has increasing value not just to the courts but to society at large. To deliver that value, however, the expert must be truly expert, impartial, objective, and qualified to shoulder the responsibility that accompanies authority. The "expert" who is inept, ill-prepared, terrified, overly defensive, or in over his or her head helps no one.

Attorneys, judges, and mental health professionals are becoming more familiar with each others' roles, functions, skills, and limitations. Perhaps the greater collaboration bound to result will mitigate the conflict, anxiety, and even disdain that has marked some of their dealings in the past. Each court officer and mental health professional can benefit from the expertise and professionalism of the other. That which is "foreign" need not be frightening or a target for derision. Rather, it can challenge one's search for greater understanding.

REFERENCES

Durham vs. U. S., 214 F. 2nd 862 (DC Cir.), 1954.

Frye vs. U. S., 293 F. 1013 (DC Cir.), 1923.

Groth, A. N. and Birnbaum, H. Jean. *Men Who Rape: The Psychology of the Offender.* New York: Plenum, 1970.

Groth, A. N. and Birnbaum, H. Jean, "Adult Sexual Orientation and the Attraction to Underage Persons," *Architecture of Sexual Behavior,* Vol. 7, No. 3, 175–81, 1978.

Hermann, D. H. J. *The Insanity Defense: Philosophical, Historical, and Legal Perspectives.* Springfield, IL: Charles C Thomas, 1983.

Jenkins vs. U. S., 307 F. 2nd 637 (DC Cir.), 1962.

McDonald vs. U. S., 312 F. 2nd 847 (DC Cir.), 1962.

Melton, G. B., Petrila, J., Poythress, N. G., and Slobogin, C. *Psychological Evaluations for the Courts.* New York: The Guilford Press, 1987.

Schneidman, E. (ed.) *Suicidology: Contemporary Developments.* New York: Grune and Stratton, 1976.

U. S. vs. Brawner, 471 F. 2nd 969 (DC Cir.), 1972.

Chapter 2

THE COURT SYSTEM

Most of us recall from school-room discussions that the court system was designed to be both efficient and fair. It attempts to divide judicial matters according to clear-cut jurisdictions and provide appeal for unjust decisions and procedural errors. Beyond these basic principles, the particulars of the court system can be puzzling, especially to someone who crosses state lines. State court systems, like the federal system, are organized in layers, and each successively higher court has some jurisdiction over the lower ones. However, names of courts are not consistent from state to state. For example, California's Superior Court is basically the equivalent of Kansas's District Court and Florida's and Missouri's Circuit Courts. As a consequence, we will talk generally about layers and their functions and refer readers to descriptions of their states' court names.

The Municipal Court

At the lowest level is the municipal court, which hears violations of city ordinances such as traffic tickets, dogs violating leash laws, and other minor disputes. The jurisdiction of the municipal court is limited to matters covered by city code and is therefore quite narrow.

The State Courts

The next level is the state court, which hears issues covered by state law. Each state court has jurisdiction over a county or other defined area and is often housed in the county courthouse. As a result, and to add to the confusion, state courts are often referred to as "county" courts.

State courts usually have a number of divisions. Civil divisions hear matters of divorce and custody and civil lawsuits such as contract disputes. Criminal divisions hear matters in violation of state law, including state felony and some misdemeanor charges. (Misdemeanors are relatively minor charges usually with limited fines or terms of incarceration—a year or less in the county jail—as maximum penalties. Felonies, in contrast, are more serious crimes, such as arson, murder, and rape, with more severe penalties.)

Two more divisions hear specialized matters. The probate court handles matters involving wills, estates, and civil competency. The juvenile court, basically a "family" court, hears matters involving juveniles, and, as we discuss further in Chapter 11, takes as its charge protecting the interests of those who come before it.

Above these courts in some states is a court of appeals or appellate court, which may choose to (but does not have to) review a decision made by a lower court. Appellate courts do not re-try cases; they review records and hear legal arguments. If they find "reversible error" in a lower court's action, they can remand the case to the trial court for review or retrial. An appellate court may also issue a *writ of certiorari* to shift a case into the higher state court or into the federal system.

Although it is unusual, several state court divisions and more than one level may be involved in a single case. Consider a hypothetical case in which a child suffers confirmed felony sexual abuse by one of his divorcing parents. The juvenile court may take jurisdiction over the child. Its mission is to protect the child from further harm and can, for example, order foster home placement or even severance of parental rights. (This circumstance is different from that heard in a civil court custody dispute; in the latter, endangerment is usually not at issue.) The state civil court will hear the divorce action itself. The state criminal court will hear the criminal child abuse charges.

Complicated enough? Imagine the results if the parent who did not commit the abuse is suspected of colluding with the abusive parent. Now, both parents face criminal charges. Imagine that the requisite level of proof in criminal matters (95% or more of the evidence) leads to a conclusion "beyond a reasonable doubt" that the abusive parent is guilty and deserving of sentence to prison. The nonabusive parent is found not guilty (not the same as "innocent"), but because the evidence for placing the child in foster care is "clear and convincing" (75% or more), the nonabusive parent can not regain custody of the child. Not surprisingly, aspects of the case are likely to be appealed, and complicated litigation could go on for years.

Standing over the state appellate court is the highest state court, usually but not always known as the state supreme court. If an intermediate appellate court does not exist, the supreme court hears appeals from the district or circuit courts. Appeals to decisions made in the state supreme court are heard in the federal court system and most likely address Constitutional issues.

The Federal Courts

Like the state court system, the federal court system is tiered, and it is in the lowest of the federal courts, the 94 United States District Courts, that most trials occur. In addition to Constitutional matters they hear violations of federal criminal law. These include intra-state transportation of contraband materials, bank robbery, treason, crimes against federal agents, and crimes committed on federal property (such as American Indian reservations). Note that homicide is not a federal crime unless the victim is a federal agent or the crime occurs on federal property.

Most of the cases that come to federal courts are civil proceedings rather than criminal prosecutions. These include trade and patent disputes and federal rules violations (illegal dumping or FCC violations, for example). Federal civil courts may also hear disputes between principals from different states contesting an issue of $50,000 or more. Federal courts decide such cases when petitioned to do so ostensibly to avoid any bias in trying the case in one of the litigant's states, and they base their decisions on governing state law. The federal system also has specialized courts to hear special matters, such as those dealing with international trade and customs laws and U. S. tax issues. Military matters are heard in "courts martial" managed by the armed services, and the U. S. claims court hears suits against the federal government.

Above the District Courts are the U. S. Courts of Appeals. They function just like state appellate courts but in matters under federal jurisdiction. Above the U. S. Courts of Appeals is the United States Supreme Court. Unlike other federal courts, which are established and eliminated by Congress, the United States Supreme Court was established by the U. S. Constitution and thereby constitutes the judicial arm of the federal government. It hears relatively few cases, but once these are decided, only the Supreme Court reversing a decision it made earlier (as on the issue of abortion with Roe vs. Wade) or a Constitutional amendment can change a ruling. Challenges to earlier decisions often come in the form of new legislation, perhaps with a slightly different focus or somewhat different language (ABA, 1990), and they supply a mechanism for keeping law in step with changing times.

Understanding the Court System

Mental health professionals who serve as expert witnesses should understand the court systems in the states they work and the federal courts served by those systems. They should know the names of the courts and the chains of command for appeals. Then, for every case in which they are involved, they should understand the path the case may be on or the path it has already taken. This background will help them converse with legal professionals about objectives and strategy and it will help them understand the ramifications of particular tactics. It is the first essential "homework" for effective expert mental health testimony.

REFERENCE

American Bar Association. *You and the Law.* Lincolnwood, IL: Publications International, 1990.

Chapter 3

THE LEGAL SYSTEM MEETS THE MENTAL HEALTH SYSTEM

A man in his thirties, recently jilted by his girlfriend for another lover, kidnaps them and threatens to kill the new boyfriend. He does so, he says, to save her from the clutches of her exploiter. To fail to protect her, or at least force her to her senses, would be wrong. He could not stand by and do nothing; he had to rescue his "damsel in distress." His former girlfriend talks him out of murdering and into surrendering, but the man feels that his mission is complete. She now sees her new boyfriend as an interloper and a cad.

The law sees the situation differently. Charged with kidnapping and aggravated assault, the defense seeks to plead insanity under the M'Naghten rule. Defense counsel contends that the defendant did not know the difference between right and wrong, or, if he did, he did not know that what he did was wrong.

Enter the expert mental health witness. Evaluation shows that the defendant clearly knew right from wrong. However, he thought that what he was doing was right. Indeed, he sees himself as a hero.

In contrast, the prosecution sees him as a potentially dangerous felon and is duty-bound to prosecute his crimes in the interests of society. The prosecution sees the defendant as accountable for his actions, cunning in his rationalization, and fully culpable in the eyes of the law.

Did the defendant really believe that what he was doing was right? Or did he make up that explanation after the fact? What did go on in the defendant's mind before, during, and after his act?

These are not easy questions. The forensic expert seeks to understand the defendant's subjective reality and his true motives. The expert tries to ferret out the possibilities of malingering or rationalizing and to determine whether the defendant suffered "mental disease or defect" at the time of the crime. If he did, the expert asks, what role did disease or defect probably play?

Probabilities and Facts

"Probably"—actually, "within reasonable medical or psychological certainty." Like scientists in other disciplines, mental health professionals talk about hypotheses, statistical norms, and levels of confidence. Seldom do scientists "prove" anything; rather, they support hypotheses with varying degrees of statistical comfort. Herein lies a difference between our legal and mental health systems. The legal system eschews probabilities and seeks "truth" and "fact." It presses for dichotomous answers: "yes"/"no," "guilty"/"not guilty." But for mental health professionals, such absolutes tend to arouse anxiety, to say the least, and their interaction with legal professionals is too often fraught with conflict—on both sides.

Fortunately for mental health professionals, they do not make absolute determinations; judges and juries are the "finders of fact." However, while legal and mental health professionals work toward such different goals, they must learn to communicate with each other. To do so requires that each understands the other's objectives, functions, and training.

Free to Choose?

Another significant difference: the legal system generally operates under the assumption that individuals have "free will." Rational people, the law believes, are free to choose and are accountable for their behavior. Science, on the other hand, tends to be deterministic. Science sees people as pushed and pulled by a variety of factors, both internal and external. Freud, who emphasized underlying "unconscious" motives for behavior, is perhaps the most notable proponent of psychic determinism. Sometimes determinants mitigate one's freedom to choose. Sometimes they suspend it. But when? How?

Taking Sides

Conflict of another sort, or disparity between the mental health professional's frame of reference and that of the legal professional, also arises from the very different roles each must play. The lawyer is the client's representative. The lawyer's job is to "advocate zealously" for the client. This advocacy sometimes contains its own set of conflicts, as for an attorney representing a parent in a custody dispute but also, at least tacitly, representing "the best interests of the child." Nevertheless, the role is defined fairly clearly. An attorney would be remiss to do less than pursue the interests of the client, and that obligation creates a role that is hardly unbiased. The mental health professional, on the other hand, is called on to be unbiased. Advocacy, except for one's own opinions, is not the domain of the expert witness.

One need only consider the litigiousness of our society, however, to see that the expert witness's role is not always clearly perceived. Not only do attorneys, judges, and juries often see the mental health professional as a "hired gun" or, even less prosaically, a "psycho-whore," but the belief that expert witnesses "take sides" is also rampant among the general public. Just as bumper stickers say, "My lawyer can beat up your lawyer," all too often lay people perceive (or hope) that "My expert can beat up your expert." Unfortunately, sometimes even the mental health professional is seduced by the desire to "win."

So, let us look at this issue of bias. Ironically, it is as critical for judges as it is for mental health professionals. Everyone has biases. No one can function without them, or every situation would be new. The person choosing among 31 flavors of ice cream could be totally immobilized without bias, having to make a completely new choice every time without a few favorites to narrow the field.

Expert for Hire?

Some of the so-called bias seen in expert witnesses derives subtly and then feeds on itself. Imagine, for example, that Lawyer Jones repeatedly calls on Dr. Smith for his opinion in custody disputes. Over time, Judge Williams hears a number of their cases. And what Judge Williams sees is Dr. Smith repeatedly supporting Lawyer Jones's positions. Aha! Obviously we have a hired gun here, the judge concludes (and yes, unfortunately, they do exist).

But wait. Let's look a little deeper. Lawyer Jones is smart and experienced, a good advocate. She also knows that Dr. Smith will talk straight with her. She knows that if she calls on him in court, he—and she—are not likely to be embarrassed by the opposition. And she knows that if Dr. Smith sees problems in her position, she may do well not to call him to the stand. In fact, she may do best to keep the case out of court.

She, like most attorneys, screens referrals. Just as she usually doesn't ask questions in court that she doesn't know the answers to already—and more about that later—she will not build a case only to have it demolished by the good doctor—and more about that later, too. In reality, Dr. Smith does not always support Ms. Jones's clients. He appears in Judge Williams's court only when his testimony strengthens a case.

So much for perceptions of bias. The key to keeping those perceptions from becoming real is to be aware of one's biases and then be able to suspend them, set them aside in the performance of one's professional duty. That ability is objectivity. The judge must interpret the law objectively and fairly. The mental health professional must similarly interpret the data objectively and fairly, in keeping with his or her training, experience, and standards of practice.

The Rules of Evidence vs. the Basis of Opinion

A final set of differences between the legal and mental health systems appears in the different methods each employs to achieve its goals. First, many legal decisions are based on decisions made in earlier, similar cases. Attorneys therefore build entire prosecutions and defenses on precedents, arguing for example that since the defendants in Cases 1 (1968), 2 (1975), and 3 (1982) were found innocent, and all three cases are like the current case, the defendant in the current case should be found innocent. This approach succeeds by dealing in generalities, eliminating the clutter of detail, and simplifying the choices that judge or jury must make. It also depersonalizes the individuals involved in the cases and ignores the differences among them.

Those individuals and their differences are precious to mental health professionals. Like all scientists, those in mental health organize their discipline with categories and types and groups and trends. As we discussed before, they like hypotheses and rules, and they like particular cases to support those rules. But they are ever mindful of the exceptions that enrich the rules (note we didn't say "prove"!), and they find those exceptions in the people they see every day. Individual uniqueness truly forms the basis of applied mental health.

The example of Cases 1, 2, and 3 leading to a decision in the current case illustrates another difference in method among legal and mental health professionals. Although we often think of attorneys as impassioned orators appealing with eloquence for the fates of their clients, such scenes appear more often on television than in real life. Most attorneys rely instead on very deliberate logic, and the rules of evidence, argument, and appeal support this approach. The defendant, a lawyer will contend, could not have committed the crime because he was home with friends when the crime occurred. The lawyer will support his claim with the concurrence of the defendant's friends, two neighbors, and the doorman in his high-rise, not with the belief that the defendant is a nice guy who wouldn't hurt a fly.

While the mental health expert will also bring more professionalism to the stand than to characterize a person as "a nice guy who wouldn't hurt a fly," the mental health professional's opinion will consider the emotional response of the subject. In criminal cases, this consideration includes the defendant's motive, subjective reality (what did the defendant perceive and believe?) and emotional state. In custody cases, the expert considers relationships within the family, emotional ties (good and bad), and parenting skills—parents' overall abilities to raise a child effectively. Such factors are not specifically set forth in law; rather, they are part of expert evaluations by mental health professionals within legal guidelines set forth by the courts and legislatures.

Considering a subject's emotional response in forming an expert opinion is not the same as bias. Rather, it is the ability to "read" and "read through" people that comes with clinical experience. It is also the blend of compassion, sympathy, and personal regard that marks the healing arts. The mental health professional must use this ability to gain rapport with and elicit feelings and perceptions from the subject, not to obscure issues. A juggling act, to be sure, but a mark of the experienced clinician. While legal professionals learn to "read" people too, as they must in screening referrals, and they can be as compassionate as anyone, they have learned to make their presentations in court deliberate exercises in logic and the presentation of evidence, and they expect expert witnesses to do the same.

The Best of Both Worlds

The legal system deals in absolutes, mental health in likelihoods. The attorney collects a fee for representing a client, the mental health professional for expertise and experience in forming an objective opinion. The courts contend that we are free to choose; clinicians claim that our choices are not so free. Attorneys value evidence and precedents; mental health professionals value evidence as well, but also the uniqueness of a particular individual. The law speaks logic, while for the mental health professional, "psycho-logic," an individual's subjective world and interpretation, rings as loud.

One can readily see that each profession may view the other with some degree of incredulity, anxiety, and even disdain. Unfortunately, such perceptions serve no one's interests, but create unnecessary tensions and confuse the real issues at hand. Mental health professionals tend to view the legal system as a hostile one. It is not. It may be foreign, but its differences call for mental health professionals to learn a new language and customs. And no, "shrinks" don't read tea leaves, hold seances, or make muddle-headed guesses. But they too have their language and customs, which the courts and attorneys calling on them would also do well to learn. Together, both must arrive at just solutions in the cases that call for their disciplines' expertise and wisdom.

Chapter 4

THE TRIAL

Many of us have learned what we know about the trial process from watching movies or television. When, by fate or design, we attend a real trial, we find that the goings-on are very different, sometimes mysterious, and even frightening. Knowing the elements of the process and their purposes helps to make trials more understandable and, eventually, quite routine.

Knowing the Players without a Scorecard

The parties involved in litigation go by different names depending on the type of case. In criminal cases, the "people," or collective citizenry, are represented by a prosecutor or district attorney and bring charges against a defendant represented by a defense attorney. In civil actions, the plaintiff brings action against the defendant, each represented by counsel. In a "no fault" divorce, a plaintiff files against a respondent. In Texas, Georgia, and New York, juries sometimes hear divorce and custody actions; judges decide these cases in other states.

In some cases, a grand jury hearing determines whether charges should be filed in a case and against whom. The federal system and about half the states provide for grand jury investigations, which involve witnesses' and sometimes experts' testimony. Grand juries are not trial juries but investigative bodies that work with the prosecuting authority to determine the likelihood of a violation of criminal law. The size of the grand jury varies from state to state.

Preparing for Trial

Trials are preceded by a period of "discovery," or preparation. During discovery, counsel for both sides may present written questions about the events of the case to each other. The recipients of these "interrogatories" must respond to them in writing. Those with knowledge about the case may be asked to complete "depositions," sworn testimony delivered out of court and recorded by a certified court reporter. During discovery, attorneys share lists of prospective witnesses, and for expert witnesses, the lists indicate which aspects of the case experts will address.

Jury trials are also preceded by jury selection. Prospective jurors undergo questioning called *voir dire* (literally, "to speak the truth") to determine their qualifications, biases, and so on. For example, jurors in a capital murder case may have to be "death qualified," that is, found to have no moral or personal objections to the death penalty *per se.* Both attorneys may reject a certain number of jurors without cause. Prospective jurors found on *voir dire* to have biases unacceptable to both attorneys are also rejected, and those who remain may be seated. Twelve members make up the jury, although this number may vary in civil cases, and one or two extras may also be seated to hear the case. They would become regular members if another juror took ill or became disqualified, preventing a mistrial for lack of a full jury.

The Trial Underway

Trials begin with both attorneys' opening statements about the case and their claims. They tell the judge and jury what they intend to prove and how they plan to go about it. Witnesses may only testify, for example, about what they know first-hand: what they saw, what they did. "Hearsay" testimony is not admissible. "Mr. Smith told me he saw Mommy kissing Santa Claus" could not be entered in a divorce case involving Mommy, although Mr. Smith might be called to establish the event. Neither are opinions permitted in testimony ("I think Mommy should not have kissed him.")—*except* from an expert witness and so long as the opinion is within the witness's area of expertise. In theory, rules of evidence and procedural requirements apply equally in all cases and govern all proceedings, although in fact they are usually a little tighter in a criminal trial than, say, a domestic relations dispute.

Following opening statements is the presentation of the prosecution or plaintiff's case. Witnesses are called to testify on behalf of the party bringing suit. Each witness is first sworn to tell the truth; thereafter, the witness is subject to a charge of perjury if he or she deliberately lies. The first set of questions put to the witness by prosecuting counsel is called "direct examination," or, simply, "direct." These are usually simple questions following a course the witness and attorney may have discussed before the trial, and are usually neither surprising nor frightening to anyone involved.

Then, defense counsel, whose job it is to discredit testimony for the prosecution, "cross examines" the witness. Cross examination may try to catch the witness in a lie or contradiction, dilute the original testimony, turn it around to favor the defense, or expose bias (as in, "Doctor, how much are you being paid for your testimony?"). Sometimes, cross examination even attempts to impugn the character of the witness. For example, an incarcerated informant may be found to have a personal interest in the outcome of the case: a judgement in this case might affect the one for which he is serving time.

Sometimes the order of presentation is reversed, as in an "affirmative" insanity defense wherein the defendant must establish insanity (see also Chapter 6). The defense then presents its arguments first; the prosecution's attempts to invalidate them follow.

The Rules of Cross Examination

Cross examination must confine itself to that which is relevant to the witness's testimony; it may not wander far from statements made under direct examination or "groundwork" laid in other testimony. Should it do so, prosecuting counsel or the judge may intervene by objecting. Sometimes the judge decides how to rule on an objection after a brief talk with both attorneys at the judge's bench. If the judge overrules the objection, the witness must answer the question but may ask to have it repeated. If the judge sustains the objection, the examining attorney may ask another question.

Although cross examination on television is often bombastic or cutting, cross examination in real trials is usually fairly refined. Neither attorney wants to anger jurors by bullying witnesses with mean-spirited rhetoric. And, in trials before judges, courtroom histrionics usually fall on deaf ears.

The Trial Proceeds

After the cross examination, prosecuting counsel may ask additional questions called "re-direct." These may be followed by "re-cross," and then the witness is excused. This process repeats for each of the prosecution's witnesses until its case is complete, at which time the prosecution "rests." Then, the defense proceeds, attempting to refute key elements of the case against it. It calls its witnesses and conducts direct examinations of each. The prosecution cross-examines, the defense re-directs, and the prosecution re-cross examines, if necessary. After the defense rests, the prosecution has the right to call rebuttal witnesses or re-call earlier witnesses to rebut elements of the defense. Expert witnesses may be re-called or, although it is rare, called only as rebuttal witnesses when the need arises. More likely, the expert rebuttal witness will be a different expert than the one who first testified in the main body of the trial, even if the issues are different. Legal professionals often choose this course of action thinking that if the original witness was not "heard" the first time, he or she won't be heard a second time.

Timing Is Everything

Throughout the trial, both attorneys try to present their cases in logical, evolving order, systematically developing each aspect to give the greatest credence to the whole and the best flow to the arguments. Witnesses are usually scheduled so that their testimony contributes to this development. However, occasionally a witness must appear out of order because he or she can not testify at another time. Expert witnesses often have trouble scheduling court testimony around other professional obligations and sometimes ask to be heard at times other than those proposed. They should bear in mind that appearing at times convenient for them can require restructuring parts of a case or result in less-than-effective testimony, since judge and jury are not prepared for what they have to say. Working with the attorney to appear at the most appropriate point in a case is usually not that difficult and is in everyone's best interests. Of course, cases do not always proceed as expected, and witnesses may find themselves called earlier or later than anyone had planned. Expert witnesses should try to accomodate these changes as graciously as possible. When they spend more time waiting in the hallway or witness room than they had hoped, expert witnesses also do well to remember that they are being paid for their time, not their testimony, and they should take care not to discuss the case with other witnesses to help waiting time pass more quickly.

Concluding the Trial

When all testimony concludes, each attorney offers a closing statement to sum up the case and argue for his or her side. These statements are limited to a review of and conclusions from evidence presented in the case. However, and here television has it right, they offer opportunities for eloquent and impassioned appeals. Then, the judge sends the jury off to deliberate with specific instructions to return with a verdict for each charge against the defendant. Sometimes the jury must decide among several options, for example first degree murder or second degree homicide or voluntary manslaughter. The judge's instructions define the options and outline the criteria the jury should use to reach its verdict.

In most criminal trials, convictions must be unanimous: all jurors must agree. In some matters, however, laws decree that fewer than all jurors can render viable verdicts. The 1992 Wisconsin trial of serial killer Jeffrey Dahmer, for example, required only ten jurors to decide Dahmer's sanity.

Sometimes jurors are individually polled in the courtroom to affirm their consensus. If jurors can not agree, the jury is described as "hung," and the case can be retried, although it does not have to be. Judges rule on motions for retrial. The guarantee against double jeopardy, being tried twice for the same crime, does not apply to retrials, for because the first trial did not result in a verdict, it is not regarded as a trial.

Sentencing

In a criminal trial, sentencing may follow receipt of the jury's conviction or it may be postponed until a separate sentencing hearing. If a separate hearing occurs, information relevant to the severity of the crime or mitigation of the sentence may be presented. Expert mental health witnesses are sometimes called at this point to make a pre-sentence evaluation of the defendant. The court may also consider information from probation, parole, court services officers, and others in deciding the defendant's fate.

Few Surprises

Barring "continuances," or requests for more time agreed to by the court and both sides, most trials are straightforward and reasonably swift. And, as this outline suggests, they have a very predictable structure, one that begins with an "introduction," proceeds with a "body," and ends with a "conclusion"—not much different than what we learned in composition courses about effective writing or in speech classes about effective presentations. In fact, the country preacher's wisdom, "tell 'em what you're going to tell 'em, tell 'em, and tell 'em what you told 'em," usually prevails. The result is the forum we have come to expect as fair, impartial and, by Perry Mason's standards, often quite routine.

Chapter 5

TESTS, MEASUREMENTS, AND THE COURTS

Psychological tests are methods of sampling behavior under standard conditions, usually with means for comparing them to objective, statistically defined norms. We often hear psychological tests discussed as if they were somehow magically able to tell us everything we want to know about someone and with very little error. Unfortunately, that is not the case. Compared to measurement in, say, physics or engineering, measurement in psychology is relatively imprecise. Therefore, tests are commonly given in batteries or groups so results can be cross-checked and errors reduced. And, just as with many medical tests, psychological test results must be interpreted. Interpreting a test requires knowing how the test works, its norms, the context in which it was given, the history of the subject, and psychological theory and research. Administered and interpreted appropriately, psychological tests add valuable information to psychological evaluations. Some legal analysts, however, do not agree.

The Value of Psychological Tests in Court

Faust and Ziskin (1988), for example, are quick to point out the deficiencies of many psychological instruments currently used in legal matters. They favor an actuarial approach to their use, one which compares results only to statistical norms and makes no further interpretation. If research shows, for example, that 80% of individuals with a certain score on a particular test are depressed, and a particular subject achieves that score, an actuarial approach would conclude that the subject has an 80% probability of being depressed and end the interpretation there.

For a more detailed discussion of this point of view, please also consult *Coping with Psychiatric and Psychological Testimony* by Faust and Ziskin, 1988. Faust's and Ziskin's disparagement of psychological and psychiatric expertise is neither a generally accepted "minority opinion" (Brodsky, 1991) nor, by their own admission, a scientifically objective conclusion. Indeed, Faust and Ziskin acknowledge that their work "consists almost entirely of literature which negates the expertise of mental health professionals" (Brodsky, 1989) while admitting the existence of supportive literature they consider "largely irrelevant from a legal context" (Ziskin and Faust, 1988).

Other authors, notably Matarazzo (1990), distinguish between psychological testing and psychological assessment. Assessment, they claim, extends substantially beyond the simple testing and statistical reporting of test results. As Matarazzo puts it, "Assessment . . . is a highly complex operation that involves extracting diagnostic meaning from an individual's personal history and objectively recorded test scores. Rather than being totally objective, assessment involves a subjective component. Specifically, it is the activity of a licensed professional, an artisan familiar with the accumulated findings of his or her young science, who in each instance uses tests, techniques, and a strategy that, whereas also identifying possible deficits, maximizes the chances of discovering each client's full ability and true potential." (1990)

We agree with Matarazzo. The "subjective component" to which he refers is neither bias nor hunch. It is the same judgment that governs the practice of any learned profession, whether that be medicine, law, engineering, or architecture. Its bases are scientific research and knowledge accumulated from training and experience. There is a tremendous array of tests that measure a very broad spectrum of skills and abilities and can be compared to statistical norms. There is also a variety of other instruments such as questionnaires and inventories that may not have the kind of statistical norming as "true" psychological tests but which are, nevertheless, very useful. The devices that are available, why we use them, and how we can use them to best advantage are the subjects of this discussion.

Types of Psychological Tests

In broadest terms, we speak of two categories of psychological tests: objective and projective tests. An objective test is one that is clearly statistically normed and lends itself well to actuarial prediction. Sometimes objective tests are scored by computer to produce arrays of probability statements from individuals' responses to test items. Most common among these is the Minnesota Multiphasic Personality Inventory, or MMPI. The MMPI also has a set of "validity" scales that detect various response sets to being tested. Two detect tendencies to "fake good" or present oneself in an overly favorable light: the L scale, which shows up relatively naive, usually transparent tendencies to fake good, and the K scale, which detects more subtle and sophisticated attempts. The K scale is the latest validity scale to be developed; it statistically corrects a number of scales to increase their sensitivity and subtly measure variables such as defensiveness and deliberate attempts to play down normal human foibles. A third validity scale, the F scale, similiarly measures attempts to "fake bad" or exaggerate symptoms.

However, no matter how "objective" such tests results appear to be, it is the responsibility of the clinician to review their results in light of other data, theory, and experience. Interpreting some MMPI scales, for example, must take into account the context in which the test is being administered. We would expect a parent taking the MMPI during a custody dispute to put his or her best psychological foot forward—and show a relatively high K scale score. A depressed person seeking help might also show a high K scale score, but that person's "faking good" would probably reflect defensiveness about admitting to inner conflict. Similarly, a high score on the MMPI's measure of paranoia will probably have a very different meaning for an incarcerated person than for a person in a clinical or non-forensic setting.

In contrast to objective tests, which offer a finite number of responses to each item, "projective" tests—the most famous of which is the Rorschach or "ink blot"—present ambiguous or partly ambiguous stimuli to which subjects are asked to respond. A subject may be asked to describe what an image looks like or what it might be, or may be asked to tell a story about a picture or end a sentence from a beginning "stem." Projective tests are based on the assumption that, when asked to structure or define an ambiguous stimulus, an individual has to reach within him or herself to respond and will in so doing reveal information about his or her perceptions, experience, or inner life. Sometimes responses to projective tests are interpreted informally, based on clinical experience, personality theory, and knowledge of common and uncommon responses to such tests. Many projective tests—notably the Rorschach—also have "scoring" systems for coding responses and comparing them to normative data.

In addition to objective and projective tests, other devices provide information about a person not just through the responses he or she gives to individual items but also through the patterns of responses to those items, patterns which can reveal his or her approach to the assessment, personal style, and so on. Such devices are commonly called "face valid"; that is, they measure what they superficially appear to measure. Asking a person if he cries a lot for no apparent reason, for example, is a face-valid question about depression. A subject who completes the stem "I hate . . . " with "my mother." may also be making a face-valid statement, although its implications must be clarified with other information about the subject.

The Benefits of Using Psychological Tests in Forensic Assessments

We use psychological tests in the legal system for a number of reasons. First, tests allow the mental health professional to collect a great deal of relevant information in an organized fashion and a small amount of time. In short, they are efficient. They also allow us to compare an individual's responses not just with broader statistical norms but also with other portions of the test battery. Finally, tests may provide information about the individual's approach to the assessment itself, information that is likely to be germane to the assessment and to the courts. Is the individual minimizing difficulties? Exaggerating them? Is there evidence of malingering? If so, what is its extent?

Malingering—presenting oneself falsely—can arise in a variety of contexts, and it is not uncommon. It should be distinguished from Munchausen's syndrome. (The American Psychiatric Association's *Diagnostic and Statistical Manual of Mental Disorders,* third edition, known as the DSM III–R, refers to Munchausen's syndrome as a "factitious disorder," especially when it involves manufactured non-physical symptoms. Note that the DSM–III–R is sometimes called the diagnostic "Bible" of the mental health professions and is actually a set of guidelines rather than rigid criteria to help in assessing mental disorders.) Munchausen's syndrome is a long-recognized condition in which the patient intentionally tries to present him or herself as physically or psychologically ill but is unconsciously motivated to do so. The sufferer of Munchausen's syndrome seeks to gain attention, gratify masochistic urges, or derive other secondary gains by assuming the role of a sick person. While malingering also involves the voluntary production or presentation of symptoms, the malingerer is consciously attempting to accomplish a specific goal. The child, for example, who "lost" his non-completed homework and pleads feeling sick is a well-known malingerer. In assessing malingering, then, one of the prime factors a clinician will look for is motivation.

The potential for malingering is almost always present in forensic cases, and the clinician should always look out for it, whether motivation to avoid or mitigate a jail term, collect insurance payments, prevail in a personal injury suit, or simply gain preferential treatment. Unfortunately, there is no simple way to determine whether an individual is malingering, but there are a several signs which can point to the condition. Malingerers tend to over-report or exaggerate symptoms, sometimes to the point of being ridiculous. Sometimes the symptoms are inconsistent; they add up to an implausible range of disorders rather than to a single legitimate one.

Test results can help spot the malingerer. In fact, some psychological tests are "rigged" to detect various types of faking. Best known among these is the MMPI. We discussed its L, K, and F scales earlier. In addition to the F scale, which measures tendencies to "fake bad," the MMPI also offers the F–K index, which with a raw score of 15 or greater can point to potential malingering. Because tendencies the F scale and F–K index detect may also be failures to understand test items and elements of acute emotional distress, they again must be interpreted carefully and in conjunction with other data, but they can help to spot the malingerer.

Sometimes not the responses to test items themselves but patterns of responding point up malingering. "Almost correct" or implausible answers to items on the Wechsler Intelligence Scales, for example, suggest conditions that warrant further exploration. Likewise, small and inhibited Bender drawings (geometric designs) may tip off malingering.

Another way to detect malingering is to suggest symptoms, slowly moving farther and farther afield of a bona fide syndrome, to see if the individual claims inconsistent or implausible symptoms. In one case, a defendant claiming headaches and amnesia was eventually led to tell a resourceful and tenacious examiner that his hair hurt. So much for the rest of his complaints, as the case turned out.

Making the Best Use of Psychological Tests

So far, we've discussed the kinds of tests that exist and why they are used in forensic settings. Finally, how to guarantee their best use? The first step is using the "best" and most appropriate tests. The most valuable meet three criteria.

The first measure of a test is its validity, whether it tests what it is supposed to test. For example, does the test that purports to measure personality do so? Does the intelligence test really measure intelligence? One of the better-known and early, invalid attempts to measure personality was devised by Franz Gall. Gall, assuming that skull contours reflect brain contours and brain contours reveal information about the personality, measured bumps on the head. Similarly, we could measure head size in an attempt to assess intellect, but, despite all the statistics our efforts could produce, we would still have an invalid test.

Second, the best tests are reliable. Reliability describes the test's likelihood of yielding consistent results each time it is used; its opposite is the "rubber ruler." Without reliability, comparing test results is meaningless.

All measurement includes some degree of error. Under extremes of temperature, even a metal ruler is a "rubber ruler," for it expands and contracts under heat and cold. For most things we measure with a metal ruler, its margin of error is acceptable. Similarly, although psychological tests measure less precisely than rulers and our errors in measurement are therefore greater, the best psychological tests' reliabilities fall within acceptable limits. For example, IQ scores of 115 and 119 obtained a year apart are probably within reasonable limits of reliability, considering the variables in question, while scores of 115 and 130 a year apart are not if the discrepancy is a function of the test, not some other intervening condition.

Third, the test should be relevant: not just a good test, but appropriate in a particular case. A test demonstrating clerical aptitude, for example, might be valid and reliable, but it may not be relevant in determining custody or sanity. However, relevance does not require that the test fully address the question at hand. An IQ test, for example, might be useful in determining competency to manage one's affairs although it could not by itself fully inform that determination. Rather, it would be a part of a battery, or group, of devices, used together in an assessment.

In fact, the "best" test in a forensic evaluation, as in clinical and other evaluations, is usually not a single test but a battery of tests. Batteries allow us to measure wider ranges of attributes than single instruments do. And, because we can compare the results of one test to those of another and check for inconsistencies, batteries also help detect errors in interpretation and help spot the malingerer.

When we use tests in a battery, we can apply a fourth criterion to judge their effectiveness, and that is "incremental validity." Put simply, each test must add to the overall validity of the battery, supplying additional information, compensating for potential error in another test, or providing results to which other results can be compared. A test that does not enhance the usefulness of the battery should be considered carefully; it may just be a waste of time.

A full psychological evaluation has a variety of components, tests—even batteries of tests—being only one. Observations of behavior, collateral information such as history, hospital records, police reports, and so on, are also significant resources in the forensic evaluation.

Psychological tests help the clinician reach conclusions, but they do not tell the clinician what conclusions to reach. Indeed, it is incumbent upon the clinician to determine how much credence to give test data, to interpret it in light of potential malingering, evasive mind set, or other spurious motivations, and to integrate it with and interpret it in the context of other available and relevant information. Used within these guidelines, psychological tests can be an efficient, objective, and rich source of information.

REFERENCES

American Psychiatric Association. *Diagnostic and Statistical Manual of Mental Disorders,* Third Edition. Washington, DC: American Psychiatric Association, 1987.

Brodsky, S. L. "Advocacy in the Guise of Scientific Objectivity: An Examination of Faust and Ziskin," *Computers and Human Behavior,* Vol. 5, 261–4, 1989.

Brodsky, S. L. *Testifying in Court: Guidelines and Maxims for the Expert Witness.* Washington, DC: American Psychological Association, 1991.

Faust, D. and Ziskin, J. "The Expert Witness in Psychology and Psychiatry," *Science,* Vol. 241, 31–35, 1988.

Matarazzo, J. "Psychological Assessment Versus Psychological Testing," *American Psychologist,* Vol. 45, 999–1017, 1990.

Ziskin, J. and Faust, D. *Coping with Psychiatric and Psychological Testimony.* Venice, CA: Law and Psychology Press, 1988.

Section II
EVALUATIONS IN CRIMINAL ACTIONS

Chapter 6

INSANITY AND DIMINISHED CAPACITY

The History of the Insanity Defense

Chapter 1 introduced the concept of *mens rea,* or "guilty mind," and its relationship to defenses based on insanity and diminished capacity to be responsible for one's acts. As Chapter 1 notes, one of the earliest attempts to define responsibility for one's actions was the M'Naghten rule, but its narrowness made the successful use of the insanity defense difficult. Few attorneys could even create "reasonable doubts" in the minds of jurors, for under M'Naghten, a defendant could be flagrantly psychotic but not the least bit insane.

The Durham, or "product," rule, also already discussed, likewise presented as many problems as it solved. It permitted substantially more latitude than the M'Naghten rule, but it failed to provide specific criteria with which jurors could assess expert testimony. Presented with opposing interpretations of what constituted mental disease or defect sufficient to produce a crime, and without guidelines to evaluate the opinions, jurors only became confused. Often they resolved their confusion by ignoring expert testimony on both sides and looking to other evidence, even intuition, to decide.

Discarded by U. S. vs. Brawner (1972), the Durham rule gave way to the American Law Institute model penal code. Here, in effect, the so-called volition prong was added to the M'Naghten rule to excuse responsibility if the individual was "incapable of conforming his conduct to the requirements of law" (Goldstein, 1967). Excepted from the definition of "mental disease or defect" was abnormality manifested only by repeated criminal or other anti-social conduct.

The volition prong arose from the notion of "irresistible impulse" in an 1834 Ohio case and was confirmed in Parsons vs. State (1887) and Davis vs. U. S. (1897). However, irresistible impulse excludes the issue of "volitional insanity." So-called volitional insanity, for example the ingestion of drugs or alcohol to the point of loss of control, is usually excluded as the basis for an insanity defense, particularly in the absence of the prerequisite "mental disease or defect." Thus, someone committing a homicide while intoxicated, for example, would probably not be able to establish a defense of insanity since he or she had a choice to become drunk and exercised that choice.

Once the question of insanity was introduced and accepted as a consideration for the jury, it was usually incumbent on the prosecution to establish sanity "beyond a reasonable doubt." That is, once the *presumption* of sanity was successfully rebutted to the court, the burden of proof shifted to the prosecution. In many jurisdictions, this has changed, and insanity has become an "affirmative defense." It must be proven by the defense, not disproven by the prosecution. As of 1985, 38 states placed the burden of proof in an insanity plea on the defense, while the others require the state to establish, at the statutory level of proof required by that state, that the defendant was sane once the insanity defense was accepted by the court (Callahan, et al., 1987).

The Pressure of Public Opinion

Not only is the insanity defense a complicated legal tactic, but it is a highly charged topic as well. Public opinion rages about it, opinion formed from just a few sensational cases. The most widely publicized was that of John Hinkley, judged "not guilty by reason of insanity" of attempting to assassinate President Ronald Reagan. The case raised an enormous popular outcry, apparently because of the phrase "not guilty," which suggests to many that the defendant goes free. In reality, nothing could be farther from the truth. Those found not guilty by reason of insanity, or "NGRI," as it is sometimes abbreviated, are not immediately released from custody. Hinkley, for example, is incarcerated to this day.

In fact, in past years, many individuals judged NGRI have been confined far longer than they would have been had they been judged guilty of the very same crime. Excessive incarcerations used to occur when individuals judged insane were held within the civil system of mental hospitals, sometimes with no provisions for review and release, rather than the judicial system, which at least usually recognizes the right of parole. The latter is no longer the case, however. Involuntary commitments must be reviewed regularly and individuals can no longer be "stored" in hospitals. In Rouse vs. Cameron (1966), the court held that the right to treatment was a constitutional right. Furthermore, in 1992, the court ruled that officials must release a formerly insane defendant whose mental illness has been cured, even if he or she remains a danger to the community (Louisiana vs. Foucha, 1984). In this case, the defendant was found not guilty by reason of insanity. Four years later, a panel of state psychiatrists recommended his release because Foucha was in "good shape" mentally. However, the panel also commented that they would "not feel comfortable certifying that he would not be a danger to himself or others." Foucha's release was not approved by a trial judge because of his potential "dangerousness," but the Supreme Court held that Foucha had committed no crime and therefore was being held in violation of his constitutional rights.

Perhaps because many believe that criminals "get off" with NGRI defenses—and some would interpret cases such as Foucha's as support for that belief—such defenses often receive a great deal of publicity, particularly cases as notorious as the Hinkley case. As a consequence, the public perceives NGRI defenses to be far more common than they actually are. A Wyoming study, for example, found that the average citizen believed the insanity defense to be used in 43% of all cases and to be successful 38% of the time (Pasewark, Seidenzahl, and Pantle, 1981). Even legislators guessed that the insanity defense is asserted in 21% of all cases. In fact, the Wyoming study found the defense used in less than one half of one percent of all cases and successful in only one case in two years. Other studies find different incidences of the defense, but all agree that the defense is both seldom used and rarely successful: it is probably used in less than 1% of all felony cases, and it probably succeeds at most one time in four. In other words, its actual importance is far less than its perceived effect.

Attempts at Clarification

Nevertheless, the insanity defense is significant if for no other reason than that it grapples with the issues of *mens rea* and free will. Recognizing the importance of relating mental health to responsibility and free will, but recognizing also its limitations, particularly when highlighted in a case such as Hinkley's, the federal government and a number of states have revised their statutes governing it. Some, including Michigan, offer a plea of "guilty but mentally ill." Defendants found guilty but mentally ill are treated and may then be returned to prison to serve out any remaining time on their sentences. In addition to this means of reducing popular fears that criminals are "getting off" with defenses of insanity, some states such as Oregon keep jurisdiction within the criminal system for at least the term of a sentence rather than turning jurisdiction completely over to the civil system.

Some states bifurcate or split the trial to address the question of guilt or innocence first and, if the defendant is found guilty, the question of insanity second. The Jeffrey Dahmer case in Wisconsin (1992) played a variation on this theme. Dahmer, accused of homosexual assault, torture, and murder, including the dissection of a number of his victims and the preservation of some of their body parts, entered a plea of guilty to avoid facing a jury trial to decide his guilt or innocence. The case moved immediately to the second phase, a decision on his sanity. As it turned out, the defense failed to prove his insanity, and Dahmer was sentenced on the basis of his guilty plea.

Twenty-one states still use some variation of the M'Naghten rule and 22 the ALI standard (Ogloff, 1991). According to Ogloff, 34 states require the defendant to prove insanity with a "preponderance of evidence" (at least 51% of evidence favoring the defense) while two require "clear and convincing evidence" (about 75%). The remaining states require proof beyond a reasonable doubt (about 95% of the evidence favoring the prosecution's case).

States' varying requirements serve no one very well. In a well-publicized case in Kansas, the mother of a 19-year-old put unrelenting pressure on her son over a long period of time to do away with a younger step son whom the mother could reportedly not stand. The family was highly dysfunctional and, with time, the 19-year-old wore down and agreed to take care of his mother's problem. He and a friend took the step-brother out into the country and shot him. His defense was predicated on insanity under the M'Naghten standard, but both the examination and other data revealed little basis for concluding that he did not know the difference between right and wrong or that what he was doing was wrong. However, had the crime been committed a county away in a neighboring state, one governed by the volitional prong of the ALI standard, the defendant might well have been successful in an insanity plea. The dysfunctional family circumstance, the nature of his relationship with his mother, and his vulnerability to her unrelenting pressure might well have supported the opinion that the defendant was, at the time he committed the crime, unable to conform his behavior to the requirements of law.

Theorists continue to struggle with the insanity defense and to find ways to address its problems. One option, put forth by Fingarette and

Hasse (1979), is "disability of the mind." These authors fault the split trial for preventing an individual from presenting a complete defense (including testimony about his or her mental health) at the first trial that decides guilt or innocence. Rather, they propose a single trial in which the jury assesses guilt or innocence without restrictions on the types of evidence entered. Then, if the defendant is found guilty, the jury further decides about the defendant's "disability of mind." The jury has four choices: it can determine nonculpable disability, culpable disability, nonculpable partial disability, or culpable partial disability. (Partial disability is similar to but not the same as diminished capacity, which this chapter treats next.)

Fingarette and Hasse's proposal retains the concept of *mens rea* as a means of defense and it obviates the need for two trials. Mental conditions bearing on responsibility remain the concern of the jury; conclusions are formed by the triers of fact. Although this approach has received little attention, its benefits may warrant consideration in jurisdictions dissatisfied with their current handlings of NGRI.

Another formulation deserves mention, that of a "justly responsible" test. Under this formulation, responsibility would be negated for individuals whose mental impairment is such that they can not be held "justly responsible." Fuzzy though this might seem, Rhode Island uses such a standard, and Ogloff (1991) suggests that making such a judgement is essentially what jurors do anyway under the current and varied criteria.

The Plea of Diminished Capacity

A compromise in some courts is the defense of "diminished capacity." Diminished capacity applies in crimes where the issue of specific intent is relevant, for example, in our earlier example of volitional intoxication. The individual commiting a homicide while under the influence of alcohol may not have acted with the requisite malice and forethought or "cool deliberation" required for a conviction of first degree murder, but he or she did voluntarily choose a state in which self-control was weakened. The individual may be held to a lesser degree of accountability or a reduced charge rather than the all-or-nothing condition inherent in the defense of insanity. Note that diminished capacity is not the same as partial responsibility; rather, it is full responsibility but for a lesser crime (Melton, 1987). At least 26 states allow for expert testimony to comment on state of mind as it may relate to diminished capacity, at least under some circumstances (Melton, 1987).

A fairly recent development in the criminal court system may also give further emphasis to the use of diminished capacity as a partial defense. A number of states are imposing strict sentencing guidelines on the courts, allowing judges much less leeway in determining sentences. One of the results of this mandated sentencing is likely to be a decrease in plea bargaining since there is less room to negotiate. Instead, diminished capacity may take on a new importance with the focus shifted from severity of sentence to severity of charge. Whether this occurs, only time will tell.

However, mental health professionals seem to be seeing a shift from relatively rare service in cases involving the insanity plea to more frequent use of the partial defense of diminished capacity. Thus, mental health professionals would do well to familiarize themselves with those crimes requiring "intent" and with the assessment of capacity to form intent. The mental health professional is not going to be asked if the defendant "intended" to commit a crime. Rather, the mental health expert will be asked if the defendant was *able* to form intent as defined by legal criteria. So, if a first degree homicide requires proof of "cool deliberation," the question would be whether, at the precise time of the crime, the defendant could have had the capacity to deliberate cooly, however brief that deliberation might have been. Such assessments are not simple. But they move closer toward defining the relationship of mental health to the responsibility for one's acts.

REFERENCES

Callahan, L., Mayer, C., and Steadman, H. "Insanity Defense Reform in the U. S.—Post-Hinckley," *Mental and Physical Disability Law Reporter.* Chicago, IL: American Bar Association, Volume II, No. 1, 1987.

Davis vs. U. S., 165 O. S., 373, 378 (1897).

Dusky vs. U. S., 195 F. 2d 754 (1961).

Fingariette, H. and Hasse, A. *Mental Disabilities and Criminal Responsibility.* Berkeley, CA: University of California Press, 1979.

Goldstein, A. *The Insanity Defense.* Princeton, NJ: Yale University Press, 1967.

Ogloff, V. "A Comparison of Insanity Defense Standards on Juror Decision Making," *Law and Human Behavior,* Vol. 15, No. 5, 1991.

Melton, G., Petrilla, J., Poythress, N., and Slobogin, C. *Psychological Evaluation for the Courts.* New York: The Guilford Press, 1987.

Parsons vs. State, 2 So. 854, 866–67, Alabama (1987).

Pasewark, Seidenzahl, and Pantle. "Opinions About the Insanity Plea," *Journal of Forensic Psychiatry,* Vol. 8, 1981.

Rouse vs. Cameron, 373 F 2d 451, DC Cir. (1966).
Stromberg, C., et al. *The Psychologist's Legal Handbook.* Washington, D.C.: Council for the National Register of Health Service Providers in Psychology, 1988.
U. S. vs. Brawner, 471 F. 2nd 969, DC Cir. (1972).
U. S. vs. Foucha, 60 U.S.L.W. 4359 (1992).
U. S. vs. Hinckley, 525 F. Supp. 1342, DC (1981).

Chapter 7

COMPETENCE TO STAND TRIAL ON CRIMINAL CHARGES

Mental health professionals are often called on to testify about a defendant's competence to stand trial on criminal charges. The legal criteria for competence to stand trial are set forth in Dusky vs. U. S. (1961). They require that the defendant "has sufficient present ability to consult with his lawyer with a reasonable degree of rational understanding and that he has a rational as well as a factual understanding about the proceedings against him."

The defendant's competence must be determined in any criminal case in which it is questioned, whether by the defense or the prosecution. If doubt about the defendant's competence exists but the issue is not raised by either the prosecuting or defense attorneys, the court must raise the issue (Pate vs. Robinson, 1966). If the issue is not raised, the defendant may be found to have been deprived of due process and his or her conviction overturned.

Competence to stand trial is quite different from civil competence, insanity, and diminished capacity. Civil competence describes an individual's ability to manage his or her affairs; insanity and diminished capacity describe a defendant's mental state at the time of the offense. Determining competence to stand trial, on the other hand, involves determining the individual's present capacity.

Incompetence to stand trial also does not always require the presence of mental disease, defect, or diagnosable disorder as do insanity and diminished capacity. Incompetence may result from situational variables such as intractable pain from a physical condition. Furthermore, the condition need not be permanent, and so a defendant's competence may be assessed a number of times. For example, if an individual is found incompetent to stand trial because of a flagrant psychotic condition, he or she might be remanded to a hospital for treatment. If treatment appears to be successful, the individual's competence might be assessed again, and the individual might return to the court for trial.

Components of Competence to Stand Trial

Competence to stand trial has a number of aspects. The individual must be able to understand the nature of the charges against him or her, not just in fact but in substance. That is, the individual must not just parrot back the charges he or she faces or even their potential penalties but also must appreciate what these charges mean. Moreover, the defendant must also have some understanding of the nature and purpose of court proceedings. Mere showing of a factual understanding of the proceedings is insufficient alone to establish competence (Lafferty vs. Cook, 1991). The defendant must not only understand what is likely to happen in court and how it may come about but also be able to collaborate with an attorney in constructing a defense.

Techniques for Assessing Competence to Stand Trial

To ascertain understanding of the charges and their consequences, the mental health professional might ask the defendant questions such as "What do the charges against you mean?" "How serious would you say that is?" "What exactly are they saying you did?" "What do you think could happen to you?" A defendant charged with murder, for example, might demonstrate competence to stand trial by responding that he or she is charged with killing another person, that the charges are very serious, and that he or she could be jailed for life.

In most cases, the mental health professional determining a defendant's competence evaluates the defendant's general mental status, including the abilities to test reality, establish and maintain relationships (especially with counsel), and communicate effectively. The mental health professional should also assess the defendant's ability to function under the stressful conditions of the courtroom; some individuals who fare relatively well in non-stressful, structured environments effectively fall apart under trial conditions. This response could be so extreme that it would trigger further evaluation, but the greater danger is that it would damage the defendant's cause as the trial progressed.

To determine the defendant's ability to understand the proceedings, the mental health professional asks about the roles of various individuals involved in the trial. What, for example, is the role of the defense attorney? Does the defendant have at least a general appreciation of "privileged communication" between attorney and client? What is the role of the prosecuting attorney? The judge? The jury? Does the defendant understand the significance of testimony "under oath"? He or she need not be able to define "oath" but should demonstrate an understanding of the need to be truthful.

To establish whether the defendant can aid counsel in preparing the defense, the mental health professional asks about potential witnesses and what they might say. The defendant should demonstrate an understanding of possible defenses presented by counsel and the ramifications of each. Most important, the defendant must be able to develop and maintain sufficient trust with counsel to disclose pertinent information.

A final assessment, often overlooked, is whether the accused individual is motivated to defend him or herself. Some defendants exhibit masochistic or self-punitive drives that move them consciously or unconsciously to sabotage their own cases. They are more than depressed or simply passive; they actively attempt to destroy themselves. The most dramatic examples of such people are those who falsely confess to horrendous, often well-publicized, crimes.

As discussed in Chapter 5, a variety of inventories and other instruments that do not quite qualify as "psychological tests" are still sometimes quite useful. Among these are mechanisms for assessing competence to stand trial by Lipsitt and Lalos (1983) and Grisso (1986, 1988). These instruments and procedures provide guidelines for evaluating and rating variables related to competence and can be very useful to clinicians charged with competence evaluations.

Incompetent to Stand Trial, but Free on Charges of Murder

Sometimes, competence to stand trial collides with other law to result in unusual outcomes. Consider a case, based on actual happenings, in which a person with significant mental retardation killed another person during a heated argument and was subsequently charged with second degree murder. In this case, the defendant's mental retardation raised the question of competence to stand trial.

Mental health professionals evaluated the defendant, and based on their evaluation, the defendant was judged incompetent to stand trial. Now what to do? Believing that the defendant should be punished for the crime, the prosecution tried to have him committed to a mental institution, claiming that he was dangerous to himself and others.

As discussed in Chapter 8, "dangerousness" also involves the issue of whether an individual is treatable. Precedent links competence to treatability as well: Jackson vs. Indiana (1972) states that an incompetent defendant receiving treatment can not be held for treatment indefinitely, but there must be a reasonable prospect for successful treatment within a reasonable period of time. However, if there is no substantial probability that treatment will succeed, the state must release the defendant or, if the defendant meets the criteria for involuntary civil commitment (presenting clear and imminent danger to oneself or others), civilly commit him or her. A second evaluation reported that the defendant's retardation was permanent and irreversible, with no known treatment available. Morever, the defendant was judged not dangerous. So, now we have a defendant unable to stand trial and suffering from a permanent, untreatable condition but judged no longer to be a danger to himself or others—although he has killed someone. The court has no alternative but to release him.

As much as the legal system prefers "black and white" to "shades of gray," it is confronted in such a case with a major dilemma. If the state were to try the defendant in spite of his lack of competence, he would have been denied due process, and if he were committed civilly indefinitely he would have been punished without trial. Not being treatable, he could only be "warehoused." If he can't be tried or committed, he has been given, as a practical matter, *carte blanche* to commit further criminal acts, including murder.

Thus, both the legal and mental health systems must deal with ambiguities and contradictions. Was justice served in this case? While vengeance may say "No," compassion and reason would probably say, "That's the best we could do in the interest of protecting the right to due process."

REFERENCES

Dusky vs. U. S., 195, F. 2d 754 (1961).

Grisso, T. *Competency to Stand Trial Evaluations.* Sarasota, Florida: Professional Resource Exchange, 1988.

Jackson vs. Indiana, 406 U. S. 715 (1972).

Lafferty vs. Cook, 949 F. 2d 1546 (1991).

Lipsitt, P.D. and Lelos, D. "Competency to Stand Trial Instrument." In Keller, P.A. and Ritt, L.G., eds., *Innovations in Clinical Practice: A Source Book.* Sarasota, FL: Professional Resource Exchange, Inc., Vol. II, pp. 278–284, 1983.

Pate vs. Robinson, 383 U. S. 375 (1966).

Chapter 8

PREDICTING VIOLENT BEHAVIOR

One of the major challenges facing the mental health and legal systems is predicting "dangerousness," more specifically, violent behavior. The courts use predictions of violent behavior in sentencing convicted criminals, determining eligibility for parole, considering release from involuntary commitment, and similar situations. At these times they try to protect the public while showing regard for the defendant's rights—a difficult balancing act achieved in a variety of ways. For example, Missouri statute places the burden on a person committed because of an insanity plea to a violent crime, stating that release depends on the person proving by clear and convincing evidence that he or she "does not have, and in the foreseeable future is not likely to have, a mental disease or defect rendering him dangerous to the safety of himself or others" (H. B., Mo., 568, 1991). Predicting dangerousness as an outgrowth of mental disease or defect is difficult at best, especially if we think of it as some kind of character trait rather than as the more complex interaction of psychology and circumstance.

At one extreme, we have Justice Blackmun's opinion in Barefoot vs. Estelle (1983), in which Thomas Barefoot appealed his conviction of killing a police officer and sentence to die. At the other we have psychiatric testimony in Barefoot's first trial that Barefoot was an untreatable "criminal psychopath" who would continue to be violent even in prison with a probability of "one hundred percent and absolute" (Applebaum, 1984). Blackmun rightly pointed out the inappropriateness of such absolutes, but he further called all predictions of dangerousness "wrong two times out of three," and he commented that "a layman with access to relevant statistics can do at least as well and possibly better" than an expert. Because mental health professionals are often called on to predict an individual's dangerousness, we can only hope—and work to ensure—that Blackmun overstated his opinion.

Unfounded Predictions

However, cases such as the landmark Baxtrom vs. Herald decision in 1966 and the events that followed substantiate Blackmun's belief. In 1961, Baxtrom was convicted of assaulting a police officer. He was judged mentally ill and confined to Dannemora State Hospital, where he stayed longer than his sentence required because he was "dangerous." He appealed, and the appellate decision required that he be moved to a less restrictive environment—that is, a regular state hospital. Shortly thereafter, based on Baxtrom, 966 other inmates previously judged "dangerous" were also ordered to be transferred to state hospitals. Needless to say, the hospitals were in an uproar, but the decision was made and the transfers took place.

Steadman and Cocozza (1980) published a study of these individuals. Although all but 72 had been transferred to open wards, none had caused problems during the year after their transfer. After four years, 98, or about ten percent, had been released, and eighty percent of those had committed no further crimes.

The issue of dangerousness is of particular importance because of the public's apparent perception that violent individuals are being released from institutions prematurely. While this may not happen as often as is generally believed, there are cases that make news, such as the case of Willie Horton. Horton's release from prison only to commit another homicide soon thereafter played a major role in the demise of Michael Dukakis's bid for the presidency in 1988.

To complicate matters, the landmark case of Tarasoff vs. the Regents of the University of California (1976), often called the "duty to warn" precedent, requires a therapist to warn a potential victim if a patient is likely to harm the victim in the near future or to "take whatever steps are reasonably necessary under the circumstances." While this ruling applies only in California, it has been invoked as a precedent in similar rulings in other states. One state has applied it to evaluations. Hawaii, however, has exempted court-ordered psychiatric examinations from claims based on such a precedent (Melton, et al., 1987). And, in the more recent Florida case of Boynton vs. Burglass (1991), the courts specifically rejected the "enlightened approach" of Tarasoff and added that "to impose a duty to warn... would require the psychiatrist to foresee a harm which may or may not be foreseeable, depending on the clarity of his crystal ball."

Responsible in Any Event

Nonetheless, whether mental health professionals can predict dangerousness or not, they may be responsible in some states for its consequences. That pressure can cause them to protect themselves by predicting violence more often than it is likely to occur in prognoses called "false positives." Add to this situation the low "base rate" of violence—regardless of what the headlines say, it seldom occurs in the general population and then at an irregular rate. The result is a well-intentioned but distorted view of the future.

To illustrate, let's assume that violence occurs two times in 1,000 people, a fair assumption based on earlier statistics (Megargee, 1980). Let's also assume that we have a test for dangerousness (although we don't) which is accurate 95% of the time and delivers false positives only five percent of the time. If we tested 100,000 people, we would correctly identify 190 of the 200 who were violent. But, of the 99,800 who were not violent, 4,990 would be incorrectly labeled violent—nearly 5,000 false positives. However, if we predicted that every individual would not be violent, we would make only 190 mistakes, less than four percent of the mistakes we would make with a 95%-accurate predictor.

Improving the Odds

Fortunately, there is a fallacy in this reasoning which improves our odds somewhat. That is that rarely in forensics are we dealing with a random or general population. In practice, we are dealing with a subpopulation in which individuals already show histories of violence: their base rates for violence are higher. As a consequence, we can predict future violence more frequently and more accurately. However, predicting it absolutely, as Blackmun observed, is not a realistic goal.

What is realistic? Understanding what we are trying to predict is the first step toward clarifying the contribution mental health professionals can make when asked to predict dangerousness. In fact, we are not predicting dangerousness or violence as if they were isolated character traits or psychological dysfunctions that we must somehow ferret out. Rather, we must predict dangerous *behavior,* as Megargee (1980) aptly points out. Even serial killers, for example, do not kill everyone they meet: dangerous behavior is seldom just a product of some intrapsychic dysfunction. It is an interaction between the perpetrator's psychological makeup, a complex set of situational variables, and oftentimes random events. One need only consider the all-too prevalent domestic homicides that follow the discovery of an illicit affair or the decision to divorce. Would they have occurred otherwise? And what about the uncovered affairs or decisions to divorce which both partners survive? Or, think about the situation when "good guy" meets "bad guy" in a dark alley. The potential for violence may be determined by which guy has the gun.

A System for Predicting Behavior

All of the factors that enter into an act of violence may seem to complicate predicting further violence, but in fact they can help sort it out. First, taking Blackmaun to heart, we must not confine ourselves to rendering absolute predictions, much as others might like such clarity. Rather, we should think of an evaluation for dangerousness as an assessment of risk under certain conditions. We might ask, for example, what effect a spouse's abrupt abandonment might have on an individual's deep dependency needs. What are the odds of a violent response?

Litwack and Schlesinger (1987) set forth a structure for assessing such risks. They view stimuli to violent behavior along a "motivational spectrum" ranging from primarily intrapsychic to primarily environmental factors, with five corresponding categories of motivations. At one end, with primarily intrapsychic motivators, is the "compulsive offender" whose internal forces are paramount. Such an individual might be driven by fantasies of violence or sadism with compulsions to act. At the other end, motivated primarily by elements in the environment, are offenders who act out of identification with social groups that condone violence—political extremists or gangs, for example. Between the two are those who respond violently to stressful situations, those who do not control their impulses well, and those who react explosively to gradual build-ups of tension with what Megargee (1980) calls "over-controlled hostility."

Applying this continuum requires two steps. The first is conducting a thorough assessment of the individual's intrapsychic world, a detailed evaluation of how he or she perceives, interprets, and reacts. The second is obtaining a detailed history of the individual's behavior, particularly his or her violent acts, the circumstances surrounding them, and accompanying feelings and behaviors. Analyzing the evaluation and history will answer a variety of questions. Is there a pattern of mistreating animals or other persons? A lack of empathy for victims? Is there anger, hostility, or hatred that might be mobilized? Are there violent or hostile fantasies? How does the individual handle stress? Rejection? Authority?

Is there a history of substance abuse? Of suicide attempts? Did—and does—the person have easy access to weapons? With what groups does the individual identify? Or is the individual isolated or without support? Does the individual have overwhelming fears? And, of course, is the person psychotic, pathologically jealous, or severely paranoid?

The mental health professional can often deduce patterns that suggest situations in which the individual might respond with violence. Consider the case of a patient in a psychotic manic state who became very agitated and potentially aggressive. He threatened to harm his wife and others, who, in accord with Tarasoff, were warned by the mental health professional who evaluated him and concluded that he was dangerous. The patient maintained that there was nothing wrong with him and refused treatment, so he was committed to a state hospital and placed on a regimen of lithium carbonate, a drug commonly used for manic states with excellent results. Shortly his functioning became more normal, and he was discharged since he had received treatment, was no longer dangerous, and had not committed any crime.

He was advised to continue his medication, but, like many manic patients, he apparently enjoyed at the least the early states of the manic "highs" and felt abnormal under the medication's influence. So, he stopped taking it and soon became seriously manic again. After receiving a traffic violation, he took off into what became a 100 mile-per-hour car chase, and was arrested for his act. Could these events have been predicted? Perhaps not specifically, but thoughtful consideration of his situation and the knowledge of many manic patients' response to medication would point toward his future acting out. Additional knowledge of idiosyncratic "triggers," if they existed, could refine the prediction even more.

Other patterns of violent response appear in domestic situations. The Battered Spouse syndrome, discussed in Chapter 9, often consists of repeated reactions to certain conditions. Pathological jealousy can give way to disaster. Crowding, poverty, and desperation promote violent behavior. These kinds of connections help predict dangerousness even though the prediction will not, at least for the foreseeable future, be highly precise—nor should it be presented as an absolute fact in court. Nonetheless, it can help the courts, and it will certainly be requested by them.

REFERENCES

Applebaum, P. "Hypotheticals, Psychiatric Testimony, and the Death Sentence," *Bulletin of the American Academy of Psychiatry and the Law,* Vol. 12., 169–177, 1984.

Barefoot vs. Estelle, 463 U. S. 880 (1983).

Boxtrom vs. Herald, 383 U. S. 107 (1966).

Boynton vs. Burglass, 590 So. 2d 446 (1891). Reported in *Mental Health Law Reporter,* Vol. 10, No. 3, 1992.

H. B., Mo., 568, Committment to Mental Health Facilities—Persons Acquitted by Pleading Mental Disease or Defect. Approved May 29, 1991, p. 72.

Litwack, T., and Schlesinger, L. "Assessing and Predicting Violence: Research, Law, and Applications." In Weiner, I. and Hess, A., *Handbook of Forensic Psychology,* 1987, 205–257.

Megargee, E. "The Prediction of Dangerous Behavior." In Cook, G., *The Role of the Forensic Psychologist.* Springfield, IL: Charles C Thomas, 1980, 189–203.

Melton, G., Petrila, J., Poythress, N., and Slobogin, C. *Psychological Evaluations for the Courts.* New York: The Guilford Press, 1987.

Mental Health Law Reporter, Vol. 10, No. 3, March, 1992, 24.

Steadman, H. and Cocozza, V. "The Prediction of Dangerousness—Boxtrom: A Case Study." In Cook, G., *The Role of the Forensic Psychologist.* Springfield, IL: Charles C Thomas, 1980, 204–215.

Tarasoff vs. Regents, 551 P. 2d 344 (Cal., 1976).

Chapter 9

THE BATTERED SPOUSE SYNDROME

Among the situations in which violence often escalates is the so-called Battered Spouse syndrome, a situation that all too often results in the victim killing the abuser not just to end the abuse but also to survive. In such cases, mental health professionals are often called on to attest to the victim's—now the defendant's—mental state at the time of the act.

While the Battered Spouse syndrome does not constitute a defense by itself, it forms the basis for defense in a growing number of states. The potential for the Battered Spouse syndrome to lead to homicide has been amply described by Walker (1979, 1984). She found marked similarities among cases in which women kill their abusive husbands. (We know of no cases in which the situation is reversed—the husband kills an abusive wife—although cases of husband abuse do, indeed, exist.)

The Cycle of Violence

Among those similarities are serious and escalating physical, psychological, and often sexual abuses leading to a sense of learned helplessness (Hiroto and Seligman, 1975), fear, and desperation. The Battered Spouse syndrome is characterized by a "cycle of violence" gradually building to its ultimate conclusion. The cycle consists of mounting tension, release, a partial drop in tension, contrition, and rebuilding tension. Each abusive outburst tends to be followed by a period of remorse, often quite emotional, and a firm resolve to "do better."

The abuser acts out his or her own pathology by verbally degrading the victim, increasing the victim's isolation, campaigning to undermine self-esteem and confidence, threatening and intimidation, displaying possessiveness, and attempting to gain more and more control over the victim's life through whatever tactics accomplish that goal. In tandem are increasing tension, emotional abuse, and physical violence. Beatings, sometimes resulting in broken bones and senselessness, are often foreshadowed by pushing, shoving, slapping, punching, and choking. Sexual abuse, forcing the victim to engage in acts against her (or, rarely, his) will, may increase as well. But despite the drop in tension after an abusive episode and the contrition, remorse, and resolve that follow, reform does not occur. Rather, the tension builds again, is released, and builds again, each time escalating a little more.

The Danger Zone

At some point the abuser may threaten to kill not just the victim but also their children. With the threat of death, the situation enters a zone of danger; a serious potential for homicide arises not only for the victim and children but for the abuser as well, for the victim may perceive the alternatives as "kill or be killed." And, since the children are now potential victims, the possibility for the abused spouse to escape becomes even more remote. It is not uncommon for the periods of remorse or, as Walker puts it, "loving contrition," to disappear, and there may be no respite from violence or threat. The bomb, as they say, has been armed. The victim is now a mere shell of a human being, living in fear, pain, and the realization that life may end at any time, perhaps even on a whim.

Why the Battered Spouse Stays—and Kills

How could anyone get into, or, more importantly, stay in such a situation? One obvious solution is to run, but not everyone has that option; the victim may see herself as financially and emotionally dependent on the abuser, for example, and unable to get along without him. "Where will I go? What will I do?" are questions an abused spouse often asks. Often, the victim feels she deserved the abuse and failed to be a sufficiently good wife, at least earlier in the progression. She stays with the abuser and "tries harder" hoping to become good enough and avoid future punishment—all to no avail. She may be followed, stalked—a particularly ominous sign. Whatever the particular reasons for staying with the abuser, the victim's general condition is that of emotional rubble. Learned helplessness is a state in which the sufferer comes to believe that her responses have no effect on what happens to her or those around her. Her world is happening to her; she is not a participant. And that world is deteriorating, already dangerous and out of control.

Menninger (1938) addressed this state years ago in talking about suicidal feelings, saying they could stem from partial or psychic death. And Wekstein (1979) describes individuals whose "lives are meaningless and without purpose: their affect is crippled and they are resigned to eternal nothingness. Their existence represents an exercise in futility." It is not surprising that some victims kill their abusers to put an end to this horror. But their acts are not psychological attempts to regain control or breaks out of the "helpless" trap. Rather, they are acts of desperation, grasps at survival.

Defending the Battered Spouse

After such an act, the victim's defense is not the Battered Spouse syndrome *per se* but some other defense that mitigates responsibility for the act. Often the defense is a conventional legal defense such as insanity or diminished capacity whose cause is the Battered Spouse syndrome. More recently, however, we hear of self defense, not the usual self defense arising from an imminent threat to one's life but a "delayed" response arising in defense of the "psychological self." In Ewing's words, such victims are defending "aspects of the self which give meaning and value to their lives." In short, battered spouses may commit homicide to defend against having been reduced to "a psychological state in which their continued existence will have little if any meaning or value" (Ewing, 1990).

Defending such acts by claiming diminished capacity requires testimony about the defendant's state of mind to mitigate the severity of the crime. Psychological self defense, in contrast, seeks to negate criminality by justifying the use of deadly force. Psychological self defense must establish that the defendant believed herself in clear danger of death or great bodily harm and at risk of being psychologically destroyed. The belief must be subjectively genuine—she must really have believed it—and objectively reasonable—others would agree that her belief was well-founded.

The Role of the Mental Health Expert

The expert witness may be called upon to serve several functions in supporting such a defense. First, the witness may be asked to describe the Battered Spouse syndrome, to explain the relevance of long-term abuse and violence to the present case, and to define the common characteristics of the battered and the batterer. (See further, Walker, 1984 and 1989, and Browne, 1987.) The expert may also explain why the victim could not simply leave or report the violence with hopes of ending it. Here, the critical differences between a battered and non-battered spouse, particularly their "subjective realities," apply. These are especially critical if the homicide is committed when the victim is not under immediate attack or threat—for example, when the abuser is asleep.

Other Views of the Syndrome and Its Future

The Battered Spouse syndrome is not universally accepted as a "syndrome." Morse (1990), for example, contends that if "irrationality produces the inability to leave the relationship, self-defense would not apply." But wouldn't irrationality by itself mitigate responsibility? A truly "rational" person, such reasoning goes, as viewed objectively from outside the cycle, would probably not have gotten into the mess in the first place. So, some courts do not allow expert testimony about it, while others circumscribe the admissability of such testimony. Some states, including Kansas (State vs. Stewart, 1988), require the presence of "imminent" threat. In effect, they disallow defenses when, for example, the batterer is killed while he sleeps. As a consequence, cases such as the one publicized in the television movie "The Burning Bed" are defended on the basis of insanity, not the Battered Spouse syndrome.

However, the syndrome does appear to be gaining in acceptance as a basis for the defenses we have discussed, and evidence of spouse-victim long-term cruelty and violence is often admissable in court. State vs. Hundley (1985), for example, reversed a lower court's failure to allow the jury to consider evidence of "the cruel and violent nature of the deceased toward the defendant."

As our understanding of domestic violence increases, more such links between mental health and legal responsibility will likely follow. In a number of states, authorities are reviewing the sentences of women serving time for homicide in light of a greater understanding of the effects of long term and severe abuse. The controversy continues, however. It is hard for many to understand how a woman might be so fearful that she sometimes involuntarily defecated when her husband yelled or threatened, yet she did not run away. It is hard to understand her state of mind when she shot him as he roused from a deep sleep. It is hard to understand how one woman could be abused for twenty years; then, one day, she pumped two bullets into the abuser, and went next door for coffee and a chat. Yet these cases exist while the law and psychology wrestle with how justice may best be served.

REFERENCES

Browne, A. *When Battered Women Kill.* New York: Macmillan, 1987.

Ewing, C. "Psychological Self Defense—A Proposed Justification for Battered Women Who Kill," *Law and Human Behavior,* Vol. 14, No. 6, 1990, 579–594.

Hiroto, D. and Seligman, M. "Generality of Learned Helplessness in Man," *Journal of Personality and Social Psychology,* Vol. 31, February, 1975, 311–327.

Menninger, K. *Man Against Himself.* New York: Harcourt, Brace, 1938.

Morse, S. "The Misbegotten Marriage of Soft Psychology and Bad Law," *Law and Human Behavior,* Vol. 14, No. 6, 1990, 595–618.

State vs. Hundley, 693 P. 2d 475 (Kansas, 1985).

State vs. Stewart, 763 P. 2d 572 (Kansas, 1988).

Walker, L. *The Battered Woman.* New York: Harper and Row, 1979.

Walker, L. *The Battered Woman Syndrome.* New York: Springer, 1984.

Wekstein, L. *Handbook of Suicidology: Principles, Problems, and Practices.* New York: Bruner-Mazel, 1979.

Chapter 10

CHILD ABUSE AND NEGLECT

The terms "child abuse and neglect" refer to a multitude of tragedies that result in emotional, physical, and sexual damage. Cases of abuse and neglect increased 225% nationwide from 1979 so that in 1989 they numbered 2.4 million (Riley, 1992). The mental health professional may be called on to deliver expert testimony in any of these cases, and each has its peculiar requirements. In all cases, however, the mental health professional is usually asked to assess the emotional impact of the abuse and the competence of the parents or guardians to care for, guide, and interact with the child, and in some cases of abuse to validate the abuse. Such evaluations are similar to custody evaluations (discussed in Chapter 12), and the same cautions apply. "Mental health," for example, is not the same as effective parenting, and American middle-class values are not always held by people of other socioeconomic or cultural groups. For instance, spanking might be seen as abuse by some and as an acceptable form of discipline by others. In short, the evaluator must look for evidence of effective parent/child relationships and remain sensitive to the beliefs and values of those being evaluated. Still, while it is not the sole responsibility of the mental health professional, there must be a definition of what constitutes actual abuse independent of parental values.

Emotional Abuse

Emotional abuse is particularly murky; it has ill-defined criteria and is not clearly separate from neglect. Although most experts can agree on the presence of emotional abuse in the most severe cases (for example, when children are punished by being locked in a dark shed or closet, or when they are blatantly and constantly rejected or berated), they may not agree on the presence of lesser forms of abuse. Identifying emotional abuse involves not only assessing events but also their impact on the child—clear signs, for example, of maladjustment.

Physical Abuse

Cases of physical abuse are often corroborated by medical testimony and evidence, including photographs and x-rays. But this is not always the case. A hand print on a buttock may be gone before an observer thinks to photograph it. One is thus sometimes left with having to assess the child's report, behavior, and emotional status to support or not support the charges. In one case, for example, a relative was said to have tied a young child to a bed and beat him severely, but the lack of marks and fear—indeed the eagerness—with which the child went to the relative's house and enjoyed the relationship there proved critical in the case.

Sexual Abuse

Perhaps the most difficult type of child abuse case to come before the mental health professional is sexual abuse. Estimates of its incidence vary, but many agree that one in four females and one in ten males under the age of 18 are sexually abused; others estimate one in three females and one in seven males (Masters and Johnson, 1992). Only in about 27% of sexual abuse cases is the mental health expert the first person to see the child, and in another 27% he or she is the third person to have such contact (Conte, 1988). Most often, the first contact is a social services agency worker, sometimes accompanied by a police officer. In addition, most cases of alleged sexual abuse involve members of the same family, most commonly a father and step-daughter. (Cases involving "fixated" pedophiles and "sexual psychopaths" who commit gratuitous rape, murder, or serial killings are rare and beyond the scope of this discussion. See Groth and Birnbaum, 1979, for additional information about them as necessary.)

Investigating allegations of sexual abuse and evaluating the parties involved are arduous, often frustrating tasks with a high risk of damage if one's conclusions are wrong. Couple these considerations with the emotional charge of such allegations, myths surrounding sexual abuse, a paucity of solid research into it, and the dynamics of the situation, and the picture can become a nightmare. The task is somewhat easier when clear physical evidence—semen, infection, or tissue damage—confirms the allegation, although even then the wrong person may be named the abuser or "softer" damage such as inflammation is opened to debate (Gardner, 1991).

The False Report

Complicating the picture of sexual abuse is the spectre of the false report. Many people believe that children don't lie about sexual abuse: Faller (1984) wrote, "... we know that children do not make up stories asserting they have been sexually molested. It is not in their interest to do so." The premise for this belief is really that children can not accurately report something beyond their experience or knowledge. A young child is unable to describe, for example, oral sex unless he or she was told about it, saw it, or experienced it. But comments about "bad touch" or vague descriptions of having one's genitals touched are not necessarily beyond a child's experience. Sex abuse awareness programs have increased childrens' knowledge and sophistication, and old rules of thumb may need to be tempered with caution. Most early research on the sexual abuse of children, apparently influenced by the hysteria created by the McMartin case in California (see Carlson, 1990), explored ways to establish the presence of abuse and determine the validity of accusations, although methods have changed substantially since then. The McMartin case received national attention for the number of allegations of abuse—369—and claims of bizarre events surrounding them—allegations of dead bodies being dug up and animals killed with bats—at a preschool. The case is perhaps a classic example of how not to handle such allegations, but it did bring the issue of child sexual abuse to the fore.

To assume that children never lie about sexual abuse and therefore that all accusations are valid is an unfounded leap of reasoning. Although the estimate is probably high, Dwyer (1985) estimated as many as 70% of false reports in cases linked to divorce. Most studies show fairly low incidence of false reports—5% or so—but they do exist and with apparently greater frequency in divorce and custody cases (Gardner, 1991). One should be cautious about assuming that false reports are malicious, even in custody disputes, for many uncorroborated allegations are made in good faith. Sometimes stress-related behavior precipitated by difficult situations—a masturbatory act, for example—is misconstrued as a signal of sexual abuse. And while children do not usually lie about such things maliciously, they do fabricate, embellish, and make mistakes. They can also be led to make false reports and even come to believe them themselves (Garder, 1991; Clawar and Rivlin, 1991). Indeed, there are reportedly now individuals who continue to believe, nine years later, that they were molested by Raymond Buckey at the McMartin preschool although Buckey was nowhere near the school when they were attending it.

Investigating Sexual Abuse

Sgroi *et al.* (1982), Gardner (1991), Blush and Ross (1986), and Edward and Gil (1986) have set out detailed procedures for investigating sexual abuse. Following is a synthesis and summary of their work.

First, the clinician evaluating sexual abuse should be truly expert, with the special skills and experience that such sensitive investigations require. The American Academy of Child and Adolescent Psychiatry has recommended that such evaluations be carried out by or under the direction of an appropriately trained and experienced psychologist or psychiatrist (1990).

Second, most of the behaviors exhibited by an allegedly sexually traumatized child are often not the exclusive result of sexual trauma. Anger, acting out, nightmares, and depression can be caused by a range of problems. Interpreting them, or other disturbed behavior, as the outgrowth—or, worse, proof—of sexual abuse is folly and risks overlooking their other causes. At the same time, assuming that sexual abuse has no wide-ranging effects is naive and dangerous as well.

The sexual abuse assessment should consider the child's language, demeanor, sophistication, and emotional state, just as any other assessment must. It must also evaluate the plausibility of what is being said. One only need recall the cost of investigating and trying the McMartin case—it was one of the most expensive trials in U. S. history and resulted in no convictions. In another case, a child told of his parents' sexual abusing and murdering their two-year old son—who was in fact alive and well (Gardner, 1991). These allegations were taken at face value when they were made, but a little judgment and investigation could have prevented them from going any farther. On the other hand, those who know a perpetrator may support his innocence primarily because "Uncle Ned could never do a thing like that!" Denial, even astonishment, from those who know the accused is not uncommon, and can impede progress in cases where abuse is real.

Often children who report having been sexually abused retract their stories. These instances do not make evaluators' tasks easy. However, if a child is asked by an evaluator if he or she has experienced "bad touch" by an alleged perpetrator whom a third person names and the child says "no," the denial can not be taken at face value; the child may simply be intimidated by the accuser's confrontation. On the other hand, denial or retraction may be taken by some as validation of the event. This "Catch-22" is analagous to the psychoanalytic doctrine which interprets resistance as confirmation, saying "no" when the fact is "yes."

Although psychological testing is often useful in evaluating any of the parties involved, it will not determine the presence or absence of abuse. Indeed, for the most part, abusers within the family show no characteristics unique to sexual abusiveness and most perform the same as a sizable segment of the general population on psychological tests. Nor, as we mentioned earlier, do victims show emotional symptoms unique to the crime except for sexualized behaviors that are not age-appropriate. However, typical profiles of male abusers include ineffectual social relationships, poor impulse control, marked dependency needs, rigid intellectual defenses, impaired marital relationships, underlying hostility to women, and histories of abuse as children themselves. But, to stress, concluding that someone showing some—or even all—of these characteristics is an abuser is flawed reasoning. In fact, the presumption of innocence may be compromised if a defendant is in a high-risk group (Heilbrun, 1992).

Another caveat applies to the use of anatomically correct dolls, seen by some as devices that will prompt children to talk openly about their experiences. Both the American Academy of Child and Adolescent Psychiatrists and the American Psychological Association (1991) have urged caution in their use. The former flatly states that they are unnecessary, and the latter comments that "there are currently no uniform standards for conducting interviews with the dolls." Moreover, some earlier versions of these dolls were anatomically *incorrect,* with genitals disproportionately large and likely to draw the child's attention to them. Most importantly, however, children will explore them and touch them just as they do other "new toys," perhaps penetrating a doll's orifice or orally touching a doll's genitals. These behaviors alone are not definitive, and other means must be used to validate allegations of abuse.

Erring in Favor of the Child

A final cautionary note: one sometimes hears or reads that it is better to err in favor of the safety of the child, to confirm the abuse in a borderline case rather than risk further abuse. Subjecting a child to the chance of continued abuse is, of course, tragic. But to inject such a bias is to miss other, perhaps more serious, risks.

A confirmation of sexual abuse can subject all concerned to unbelievable stresses beyond those already imposed by the abuse. The alleged perpetrator is blocked from contact with the child. In abuse within the family, if the perpetrator does not leave, the child is placed in a foster home or some other "protected" environment. The child may also be removed if the nonabusive parent is judged unlikely to protect the child or, worse, is seen to be a collaborator, if only because of passivity or denial. Charges may be filed, social service agencies including police involved, examinations conducted, and lawyers—usually including a guardian *ad litem*—engaged or appointed, and the family split, however temporarily.

Imagine a worst case. Allegations of child abuse come about in an already dysfunctional family. The mother protects the father, saying that the alleged perpetrator was not capable of such an act. The social service agency, with sanction of the juvenile court, removes the child from the home. The abuse is "confirmed" and the mother cited for collusion if not actual participation in the abuse.

A variety of legal mechanisms start into motion. Criminal charges are filed against the parents and severance proceedings begin in juvenile court, in part because no one will admit to the abuse so that a diversion program could start. The stress of the whole situation increases as various pressures put on the parents, already dysfunctional, result in separation and divorce proceedings. Three separate courts are involved, so coordination and communication problems become enormous.

Eventually, the couple is divorced, the father convicted, the mother acquitted, parental rights are severed, and the family is completely blown apart. This story illustrates that erring in the interests of protecting the child is a double-edged sword. Such a bias should have no place in the investigation of sex abuse or, for that matter, any other evaluation, for severe damage can result.

Legal consequences add to the stress and to the damage. In one case of interfamilial child abuse involving fondling but no penetration or physical evidence or damage, a father was found guilty of perpetrating the abuse. In keeping with the goal of attempting to reconstitute the family or, at least, keep it intact, a motion was made for the father to enter a diversion program and undergo treatment with the rest of the family.

However, as is often the case, the father refused to admit guilt, persisting in his claim of innocence and claiming that if abuse had taken place it had involved someone else. This was, by the way, a plausible claim, since there were other members of the family who could have been the abusers. However, the father's refusal to admit guilt was interpreted as a refusal to accept responsibility and an indication that he was untreatable. He was regarded as ineligible for the diversion program, the condition of which was his admission of guilt. Another Catch-22: guilt or innocence aside, a falsely accused perpetrator would seem to do well to admit guilt and take the diversion rather than face a jury trial, possible conviction of the basest of crimes, and extended time in prison.

Such a case occurred in Montana (Montana vs. Finley, 1992), but with an additional legal twist. An individual was convicted of molesting a seven-year-old girl. He was placed on probation on the condition that he enter into a therapeutic program, but he denied guilt and therefore could not continue in court-ordered treatment. Probation was revoked and the individual was sentenced to five years in prison. However, the Montana Supreme Court set aside the sentence, holding that the Fifth Amendment prohibits increasing the individual's sentence as a penalty for refusing to incriminate himself.

The case is now before the United States Supreme Court on the basis that the Montana high court ruling threatens the state's ability to use sex therapy programs that require individuals to admit their acts. In addition, the defendant's attorney is claiming that the defendant may also be required to face perjury charges if he confessed to events formerly denied under oath.

Bias in favor of the child assumes that sexual abuse is always traumatic. This assumption is open to question (Rosemond, 1992, Block, 1991). Surely, non-genital fondling is different than anal penetration. Yet such distinctions can get lost in therapists' zeal to protect. Moreover, feelings of betrayal may damage the child more than the abuse *per se.* No form of sexual abuse can be condoned, and the least traumatic forms can escalate. Some kind of intervention should be employed. But that intervention should be therapeutic, not traumatic. Good science, clinical judgement, and common sense must guide our response to sex abuse, one of the most serious responses and responsibilities the mental health expert can face. May we discharge that responsibility with as much sensitivity and accuracy as we can.

REFERENCES

American Academy of Child and Adolescent Psychiatrists. *Policy Statement: Guidelines for the Evaluation of Child and Adolescent Sexual Abuse.* Washington, DC: American Academy of Child and Adolescent Psychiatrists, 1990.

American Psychological Association. *Statement on the Use of Anatomically Detailed Dolls in Forensic Evaluations.* Washington, DC: American Psychological Association, 1991.

Block, T. "Rational Recovery from Childhood Sexual Abuse," *Journal of Rational Recovery,* Vol. 4, No. 1, 1981.

Blush, G. and Ross, K. *Sexual Allegations in Divorce: The SAID Syndrome.* Unpublished manuscript, 1986.

Carlson, M. "Six Years of Trial by Torture," *Time Magazine,* January 29, 1990.

Clawar, S. and Rivlin, B. *Children Held Hostage: Dealing with Programmed and Brainwashed Children.* Chicago, IL: American Bar Association, Section of Family Law, 1991.

Conte, V. "What Every Professional Should Know About Sexual Abuse of Children." Seminar held in Overland Park, Kansas, 1988.

Dwyer, M. "Sex Abuse 'Hoax' Cases Linked to Divorce." *Marriage and Divorce Today,* Vol. 11, No. 2, 1985.

Edwards, D. and Gil, E. *Breaking the Cycle: Assessment and Treatment of Child Abuse and Neglect.* Los Angeles, CA: Association for Advanced Training in the Behavioral Sciences, 1986.

Faller, K. "Is the Child Victim of Sexual Abuse Telling the Truth?" *Child Abuse and Neglect,* Vol. 8, 1984, 473–481.

Finhellar, D. *Sexually Victimized Children.* New York: MacMillan, 1979.

Gardner, R. *Sex Abuse Hysteria: Salem Witch Trials Revisited.* Cresskill, NJ: Creative Therapeutics, 1991.

Groth, N. and Birnbaum, H. *Men Who Rape: the Psychology of the Offender.* New York: Plenum, 1979.

Heilbrun, K. "The Role of Psychological Testing in Forensic Assessment," *Law and Human Behavior,* Vol. 16, No. 3, 1992.

Masters and Johnson. "Sexual Trauma Program," *The Masters and Johnson Report,* New Orleans, Vol. 1, No. 1, Winter, 1992.

Montana vs. Finley. In *Mental Health Law Reporter,* Vol. 10, No. 3, March, 1992.

Riley, M. "Corridors of Agony," *Time Magazine,* Jan. 27, 1992.

Rosemond, J. "Columnist Stands By His Molestation Reply," *Houston Chronicle,* April 9, 1992.

Sgroi, S. *Handbook of Clinical Intervention in Child Sexual Abuse.* Lexington, MA: Lexington Books, 1982.

Section III
EVALUATIONS IN CIVIL ACTIONS

Chapter 11

THE JUVENILE COURT

Perhaps the most long-standing relationship between mental health professionals and the court system has been through the juvenile court. Established in the late 19th Century, the juvenile court was charged with acting in behalf of youthful individuals. This charge has been referred to as the *parens patriae* or "state as parent" power. Thus, even though the juvenile court often deals with individuals who, were it not for their age, would be "criminals," the court is more like the family or domestic relations court.

Determining Foster Care and Severance of Parental Rights

In fact, one function of the juvenile court is to hear recommendations for placement in foster care. Termination of parental rights is based on the presence of clear and convincing evidence that continued parent-child contact would be detrimental to the child. Its detrimental impact may result from the parent's mental illness or retardation resulting in failure to provide the child proper care or control. In such cases, the parent's disability must also be shown to be ongoing and untreatable, either because treatment does not exist or because the parent will not cooperate. A parent may not be deemed "unfit" simply because of mental disability, however, and parental rights of mentally disabled persons can not be terminated automatically. Rather, the court seeks to serve the best interest of the child.

Foster care is sometimes recommended for victims of child abuse. It is rare, however, that a severance motion in a case of abuse would be heard in juvenile court if other parts of that proceeding are pending in another court. The severance motion would more likely be heard in that court.

Dealing with Juvenile Offenders

The juvenile court's other primary function is dealing with youthful offenders. By virtue of the *parens patriae* power, the juvenile court's original goal was to protect the offenders' interests while rehabilitating them and, historically, the court performed more a civil than criminal function. Children were not to be held to the same standards of accountability as adults, and so juvenile courts sought not to punish but to treat them. To avoid the stigma and consequences of criminal prosecution, juvenile records were kept private and sealed to prevent a child's record from following him or her into adulthood.

Within this system, mental health professionals were called upon to conduct evaluations not very different from other types of evaluations except for their objective: to serve as a basis for the rehabilitation and reintegration of the child into the community, to live there in a constructive and law-abiding fashion. Thus, in addition to assessing intellectual and personality variables, the mental health professional often looked at family ties and support, school performance, social interactions, relationships to community resources, affiliations with social groups, and so on.

Challenges Faced by the Juvenile Court

Melton (1987) writes that, despite their good intentions, juvenile courts failed to live up to their promise. He quotes U. S. Supreme Court Justice Abe Fortas *In re: Gault* (1967), who described juvenile courts of that day as "kangaroo courts." Gault addressed some concerns about them by establishing that juveniles were entitled to due process including right to counsel, timely notice of charges, and Fifth Amendment protection. Gault also essentially formalized the juvenile court system and emphasized the need for fair treatment, a need which had sometimes been suspended in the interests of privacy and rehabilitation. As Melton notes, however, it is difficult to reconcile the elements of due process as expressed in Gault with an emphasis on rehabilitation. And while juvenile courts try to serve both masters, the difficulty of doing that well plagues them to this day.

Juvenile courts are also witnessing an increase in crime, particularly violent crime. In some jurisdictions, as many as 80% of all cases involve youthful offenders. The remainder, mostly cases of abuse and neglect, involve youthful victims. Nationally, about 340,000 children are in some kind of foster care (Riley, 1992). The ability of the juvenile court to protect society from violent youths is limited, and the court loses jurisdiction as the child comes of age. Often, juveniles incarcerated in facilities designed for them must be released prematurely, at least in the eyes of some observers. Moreover, some juvenile institutions are unable to intervene effectively in criminal behaviors. Thus, in some cases, society prefers to try youthful offenders as adults.

While at one time the adult criminal justice system was as interested in rehabilitation as the juvenile court, the belief that most criminals could be completely rehabilitated has long gone by the board. Most people have put idealism aside and believe today that the principle reasons for incarceration in the adult criminal system are punishment and the protection of society. Unfortunately, this orientation results in locking criminals up and keeping them locked up. As a result, the United States now has the largest per capita prison population in the world (Mauer, 1992), and when juveniles are tried as adults and convicted of their crimes, they become part of this population.

Trying Juveniles as Adults

Most times, a particularly serious crime or history of repeated serious criminal behaviors will raise the issue of waiving a juvenile to be tried as an adult. Kent vs. U. S. (1966) laid out five broad categories of consideration for a waiver hearing. They are the seriousness of the offense, the prior record and character of the child, his or her pattern of living, whether the offense (usually a lesser one) is part of a repetitive pattern possibly beyond the rehabilitative powers of available facilities, and whether society's interests are best served by the child standing trial as an adult.

The State of Kansas (KSA 38-1636) also set forth criteria for determining waiver to adult court. We single these out because some make the role of the mental health professional readily apparent. The first consideration is the seriousness of the alleged offense and whether the protection of the community would seem to require prosecution as an adult. The mental health professional may be asked to address the issue of potential threat to the community. What kind of impulse control exists? What are the juvenile's motivations? Is he or she likely to harm others? Is the juvenile aggressive? Easily led? What family support is available?

The second consideration is whether the alleged offense was committed in an aggressive, violent, premeditated, or willfull manner, which raises the issue of intent (see also Chapter 6). The third consideration, and not a question for the mental health professional, is whether or not the alleged offense was committed against a person or property. The court gives greater weight to an offense against a person, especially when personal injury results from the crime. Fourth, also of interest to the mental health professional, is the number of unadjudicated or pending offenses for the defendant. Fifth is the defendant's general history, particularly the nature of previous offenses and their demonstration of antisocial behavior or patterns of physical violence. This consideration can be addressed objectively—that is, we can count up prior crimes—but the mental health professional may be asked to assess, for example, patterns of motivation, rationalization of the behavior, and elements of remorse and empathy. Sixth, and definitely the province of the mental health expert, is the assessment of the individual's sophistication or maturity in relation to the home environment, emotional attitude, pattern of living, and desire to be treated as an adult. The seventh consideration is whether there are adequate facilities and programs available to the court that are likely to intervene and rehabilitate the offender before the court's jurisdiction expires. While these facilities and programs do not require a mental health expert to identify, the expert may be asked whether they can meet the offender's needs. Finally, the hearing asks whether the interests of the offender and the community are better served by adult criminal prosecution. This effectively sums up the previous considerations: it is not exclusively an issue of mental health, but a mental health expert's opinion may be helpful to the court in making an adjudication.

So, as with other evaluations, the mental health expert may be called on to assess a young offender's personality make-up and his or her identifications and support systems. Just as with adult offenders, the juvenile offender's mental state at the time of the alleged crime may bear on motivation and criminal intent.

With the increase in child abuse and other domestic disturbances and juvenile crime and violence, the mental health professional's role in juvenile court will likely become increasingly important. Unfortunately, that role is played after the fact—the domestic disturbance or juvenile crime has occurred by the time the mental health professional becomes involved. Even if one believes that juvenile offenders can be rehabilitated to lead productive adult lives, the costs of doing that are high. Better, many agree, to prevent domestic disturbance and juvenile crime through education and easier access to treatment for children and families with problems.

REFERENCES

In re: Gault, 387 U. S. 1, 16–17 (1967).

Kent vs. U. S., 383 U. S. 541 (1966).

KSA 38-1936.

Mauer, M. "Sentencing Project," *Kansas City Star,* February 11, 1992.

Melton, G. B., Petrila, J., Poythress, N. G., and Slobogin, C. *Psychological Evaluations for the Courts.* New York: The Guilford Press, 1987.

Riley, M. "Corridors of Agony," *Time Magazine,* January 27, 1992.

Chapter 12

CUSTODY EVALUATIONS

Few crises are more wrenching than divorce, especially when the divorcing couple has children. And, although the courts view divorce as the legal termination of a marriage, there is an emotional termination as well, an emotional "divorce." The feelings of failure, loss, anger, and guilt in emotional divorce make the legal process all the more difficult. Yet, work through the process divorcing parents must. And chief among the problems they face is the question of who "gets" the kids.

This phrase suggests why the legal side of divorce is so difficult. Divorces have long been adversarial: the party suffering the greatest fault prevailed and the loser was punished with a less-than-equitable share of the wealth. Today, the most common legal bases for divorce are incompatibility and irreconcilable differences, benign ways of saying that the spouses do not get along and do not expect to. However, even the most amicable and enlightened of today's divorces are cast in the tradition of competition, and the majority continue to live it out.

Evolving Views of Custody

From ancient times until the mid-19th Century, children were viewed as chattel, or property of the father, and their custody automatically reverted to him. By the late 1800s, however, the "tender years" presumption usually awarded sole care, custody, and control to the mother unless she was found unfit. This presumption held that a child of tender years, usually seven or fewer, belonged with its mother and that fathers were superfluous in the raising of children.

However, U. S. Supreme Court decisions over the past few decades have legally recognized both sexes' fitness for tasks previously the province of one. Science has rejected the notion of "maternal instinct" in humans. By definition, instincts are complex, unlearned patterns of behavior, and humans—by dint of their sheer cognitive abilities—practice no such unlearned patterns. So, replacing the doctrine of tender years is one which serves the best interests of the child. Custody may be awarded to either parent or both.

Options for Awarding Custody

Just as the philosophy of custody has changed, so have its options. Earlier, sole custody was in effect exclusive legal and physical custody; the custodial parent could virtually banish the other from the child's life. This extreme interpretation of winning and losing gradually gave way allowing visitation for the non-custodial parent, commonly the right to see the child one day each week and every other weekend. However, the custodial parent retained full responsibility for most legal affairs affecting the child, including authorizing elective medical, dental, and other health care. The custodial parent was also responsible for providing food, clothing, shelter, and so on, usually with child support payments from the non-custodial parent.

Sole custody remains one way of determining the child's place after divorce. However, while sole custody is simple and clear-cut, it has disadvantages. The full responsibility felt by the custodial parent can become a heavy burden, and the non-custodial parent too often neglects to pay child support. With limited contact, the non-custodial parent can become a "Disneyland" mom or dad, whose time with the child is mostly devoted to entertainment. Too often even this contact disintegrates into tense dullness as fun and games get old, and sometimes the visiting parent drops out of the child's life altogether.

While sole custody usually limits visitations by the non-custodial parent, the law does not hold that a parent forfeits all rights to see the child because that parent wants to end the marriage, a claim often used to rationalize vindictive moves in court. Courts regard a parent's right to contact with a child, and *vice versa,* as a fundamental right. Only in extreme cases is that right severed or supervised contact required. Simply put, most cases involve decisions about what kind of contact will exist, not whether there will be any at all.

Split custody, a seldom-used variation, sends one or more of several children off with each parent. While this option divides the responsibilities of parenting more equitably than awarding custody of all children to one parent, separating siblings can deprive them of the support they gave each other during their parents' divorce, and it risks the greatest fragmenting of family ties. It occurs only under exceptional circumstances, as when one child persistently abuses a sibling.

A third option is joint custody, or the sharing of a child's legal and physical custody by both parents. Years before the law recognized problems with sole custody awards, many couples did, and they decided to disregard their decrees and "co-parent" even though they were divorced (Roman and Haddad, 1978). Gradually, many states changed their laws in accord with these arrangements, and today, some states even presume that joint custody will be implemented unless sound reasons argue otherwise.

Many states differentiate between joint legal custody and joint physical custody. Under joint legal custody, both parents retain the same legal prerogatives as they did before the divorce. Parents are expected to collaborate in solving problems involving the child, which should result in more harmonious relationships for all. Joint legal custody should also reduce the trips back to court to resolve a whole range of disputes. For many couples, it has achieved both goals.

Joint physical custody addresses the time the child spends with each parent, usually from one-third to one-half time. Sometimes, logistics prevent equal access; if parents live far apart, for example, they must divide their time differently. Alternating years, or even months, can whipsaw the child from one context to another, and often very young children do not fare well in "even-steven" arrangements. However, most parents who spend approximately equal time with their children have the opportunity to maintain relationships grounded in realistic patterns of activity and contribute to the children's development without the burdens of full-time, single parenting.

But joint custody also has its disadvantages. Under joint legal custody, one parent can "neutralize" the other just as he or she could while unhappily married. Breaking an impasse may require formal negotiation or further litigation. Joint physical custody presents the even more destructive potential for continuing the child manipulation that characterizes many eroding marriages. If divorced parents remain angry at each other, they may continue to expose the child to their anger, campaign to win the child to their sides, test the child's loyalties, or require the child to spy on the other parent. Regardless of the type of custody, however, once a divorce takes place, the court retains ultimate authority over the children until they reach the age of majority according to state statute, usually 18.

Klein *et al.* (1989) found that the amount of hostility continuing between parents significantly predicts a child's post-divorce adjustment:

children exposed to ongoing parental animosity tend not to adjust well over the long term. The study also found that the type of custody arrangement did not make much difference in the child's adjustment over the long term. However, longitudinal research on custody arrangements is in its early years and involves a tremendous number of variables. Therefore, joint custody awards should take into account each set of parents' abilities to carry them out rationally and responsibly. Mental health professionals can be of significant help, not just in recommending the most appropriate type of custody but also helping to implement the most effective living arrangements.

Serving the Best Interests of the Child

Given their advantages and disadvantages, which option is the best in a particular case? The law outlines the factors that serve the "best interests of the child," in some states with formal statutory language and in others simply by reference and precedent. The principal guidelines appear in the Uniform Marriage and Divorce Act of 1979:

> The court shall determine custody in accordance with the best interest of the child and shall consider all relevant factors including:
>
> 1. The age and sex of the child.
> 2. The child's relationship with parents, brothers and sisters, or anyone else who may greatly affect the child's interest.
> 3. The emotional ties between the child and the parents.
> 4. The capacity and willingness of parents to provide for the child's needs and education.
> 5. The permanence and continuity of proposed custodial environments.
> 6. The extent the parents cooperate in allowing the noncustodial parent to foster a continuing relationship with the child.
> 7. The child's adjustment to home, school, and community.
> 8. The mental and physical health of all people involved.
> 9. The wishes of the child as to his custodian.
>
> Note: a. The court shall not consider conduct of a proposed custodian that does not affect his/her relationship to the child.
> b. Custody shall not be awarded on the basis of the sex of the proposed custodian.

The stipulation that conduct not affecting the child be excluded from consideration can be construed to exempt the sexual orientation of a gay or lesbian parent, sexual conduct with partners other than the spouse if it does not directly affect the child, and a host of behaviors probably relevant to the divorce but not to parenting. However, domestic courts have wide discretion in weighing factors they deem important so long as those factors are not prohibited by the particular state's law, and this provision is construed widely as well.

Considerations in Conducting a Custody Evaluation

Applying the Uniform Marriage and Divorce Act guidelines in a particular case is the goal of the custody evaluation. Custody evaluations include the same three steps as any other type of evaluation: collecting data, assessing it, and communicating the results in a written report. However, although custody evaluations look at the overall adjustments of the parties involved, as do other evaluations, custody evaluations assess two or more people and the dynamics among them, while other evaluations may not be so complex. In addition, "mental health" is not the same as knowing effective parenting techniques, and that is not the same as practicing effective parenting techniques. Determining the first is a goal of most other evaluations; determining all three is a goal of a custody evaluation.

Finally, and to repeat, the evaluation must serve the "best interests of the child." The evaluator is not the agent of the person making the referral, paying the bill, or pressing the hardest. In fact, some wise clinicians complete custody evaluations—all forensic evaluations, for that matter—on retainers rather than promises of payment. This practice protects the evaluator from the high default rate on bills after court hearings. It also removes the appearance of subtle pressure from an outstanding bill on reporting and testifying.

Custody evaluations are also best done under specific court order, but often attorneys agree upon an examiner and no court order is issued. Sometimes one attorney requests a second evaluation by another expert, which draws the lines for the "battle of the experts." Interestingly, and contrary to popular belief, well-trained and experienced mental health professionals do not disagree much in their findings. They may recommend different remedies depending on their orientations, but most agree on what the problems are, so battles of the experts may simply double the bills.

These considerations argue for evaluators with thorough training and substantial experience. An extreme example, but one illustrating the need for sophistication, is the story of a custody recommendation ultimately turning on an observation made of the home that electrical outlets were not covered with child-proofing plugs. Surely, other variables bear more weight.

Collecting Information

Just what are those variables? The evaluation begins by clearly defining the issues at hand, by reviewing the court order if there is one, sometimes by conferring with the attorney or attorneys, and by obtaining thorough clinical histories from each parent. At a minimum, the evaluation fully assesses both parents, the child, and the interactions between parents and child. It gathers data to gauge emotional ties, the ability to parent, and the ability to meet the child's psychological needs.

Tests and Measurements in Custody Evaluations

In addition to interviewing those involved, the evaluator may use psychological tests and inventories. Gardner (1986) prefers interviews and observations of behavior, to tests and inventories, not surprising given his training and experience as a psychiatrist. However, like interviews and observations, tests simply sample behavior to form appropriate deductions. Tests can yield results to compare to norms and other criteria. Inventories measuring parenting skill, marital interaction, and personality dynamics also yield relevant information in an organized fashion, just as other psychometric instruments allow the objective assessment of lying, overly defensive response sets, and potentially inappropriate motivations. Tests and inventories do not elicit information that can't be obtained in other ways, so they are not magic, but they are efficient.

Other Sources of Information

The custody evaluation may include other significant people in the child's life—step-parents, potential step-parents, grandparents, teachers, school administrators, babysitters, pediatricians, other mental health professionals. Some evaluators interview parents' friends who serve, in effect, as "character witnesses," but that has disadvantages as well. What are the witness's motives? And, for every five or six friends who support one parent's position, five or six may support the other's, leaving the evaluator to sort them all out but likely gain little new information.

Home Studies

Home studies, in which evaluators observe children in their homes, present similar problems. Home studies reveal serious problems, such as dismally unclean conditions. They also provide more natural settings for the subjects. However, assessing the information they divulge—the second step in custody evaluations and the one we will consider next—can be very difficult, as we will discuss.

When is Enough Enough?

When collecting data, the evaluator must eventually decide where to stop. Usually, the evaluator begins to hear the same information repeated with nothing new added. Passing the point of diminishing return just means more expense for those who have commissioned the evaluation.

Making Sense of It All

The second, and probably most difficult step, is assessing the data that has been collected. Here the evaluator must determine which parent, or both, will be the most effective parent for the child. Effective parenting is an extraordinarily complex set of skills beyond the scope of this book. However, we can sum up parenting by reviewing its three components:

The Emotional/Affective Relationship. The evaluator assesses the emotional bonds, the rapport between parent and child, the "love." This component of parenting serves the child's need to receive and learn to show affection. A hostile, sterile, or otherwise negative emotional tone will not foster healthy development. However, parents don't always feel loving or calm toward their children. Children are the same. The evaluator should try to assess the balance that normally exists.

Parenting Skills. The evaluator must assess the parents' ability to care for the physical well-being of the child and attend to the child's emotional, social, and intellectual development. The evaluator must also assess the kind of role model the parent makes. In developing positive self-images, children learn more from what they see than what they are told. Responsible, reasonable parents tend to raise children who themselves become responsible, reasonable parents.

Each Parent's Contribution. Children do best with access to two effective parents. What they take from each, however, may be quite different. Fathers tend to play more, sometimes even roughly, while mothers tend to talk more to their children and be more overtly emotionally nurturing. Mothers are strong role models for their daughters and the "prototypes" of the opposite sex for their sons. The reverse is true for fathers.

A "Psychological Parent"?

Parents' different contributions conflict with the notion of the "psychological parent" put forth by Goldstein *et al.* (1973). Based primarily on psychoanalytic theory, the notion implies that principal bonding occurs with one parent, usually the mother. Because the mother usually has greater nurturing interaction, particularly with a very young child, she is more often seen as the "psychological parent." Unfortunately, this reasoning is both circular and limited. It also risks resurrecting a climate of maternal preference.

Ensuring a Fair Assessment

In reaching conclusions, the evaluator should try to support every hypothesis with at least two bits of information from the evaluation and to account for apparent contradictions, not ignore them. The evaluation's internal consistency is critical.

Earlier we mentioned the difficulty of assessing data from a home study. Home studies put subjects in familiar settings, but they put examiners in unfamiliar territories, and that increases examiners' possibilities for error. The environment familiar to the examiner—for example, his or her office—is in essence a standard context analagous to the standard administration of some tests and inventories, and it eliminates factors that can confound the evaluation. An example illustrates its value. During one home study, the young child took off and was observed in a corner of her bedroom playing with toys shortly after the evaluator arrived. Was the child fearful? Anxious? In fact, the evaluator had seen the child before in his office, where the child had had good rapport with him. At home, the child was probably not interested in hanging around for what looked like "adult talk," preferring instead to play with her toys. The child was well-adjusted and not responding negatively in any way. However, the home study alone would probably not have supported that conclusion.

One tactic for validating recommendations that also helps to prepare the report or testify in court is to try to support an opposite point of view—Parent A as the custodial parent, for example, if the data suggests custody for Parent B. This process reveals the strengths and weaknesses in both recommendations and helps the evaluator anticipate objections.

Another technique for sorting data and cross-checking findings is the Custody Quotient (CQ) technique (1987). The CQ includes a semi-structured interview and a set of scales for rating variables such as parents' abilities to meet a child's emotional needs, absence of dangers, overall parenting skills, and suitability for joint custody. The CQ is neither a test nor does it provide a totally independent review; it should not be the sole means of gathering and assessing data. The CQ is a research instrument and, as such, helps paint only part of the picture. However, it helps the clinician both organize the data and review it.

Working with Incomplete Information

What if a significant player, such as one parent, does not participate in the evaluation? This handicap precludes a "custody evaluation," but the evaluator can assess the information that is available and make recommendations, limited, but still of value to the court. For example, assessing only Parent A's relationship with a child is not enough to recommend that Parent A should receive sole custody. One of the first questions Parent B's attorney will ask is, "Well, Doctor, you haven't seen Parent B, have you? Then you don't know whether Parent B might not be the better custodial parent, do you?" The most the mental health professional can say is that Parent A's relationship with the child and ability to parent do not speak against Parent A being an effective custodial parent, and no comparison to Parent B is implied. In cases in which the child is disturbed, and his or her condition can not be explained by the evaluation of only one parent, the mental health professional may express concern and recommend further evaluation. The American Psychological Association Committee on Professional Practice and Standards is currently developing child custody evaluation guidelines which will address such issues of procedure and other concerns (*APA Monitor,* 1992).

Other Considerations

The impact of divorce varies depending on the child's age, sex, maturity, and the handling of the divorce itself. A detailed review of child development is beyond the scope of this book—and the forensic specialist testifying about custody issues must be thoroughly familiar with child development. However, to summarize, divorce early in a child's development can contribute to insecurity, fear of abandonment, loss of trust in relationships, and major overall confusion. An adolescent whose emotional development is on track is less likely to be rocked, but his or her loyalties will be tested, especially if either parent begins a new romantic relationship. Adolescents may have concerns about the viability and permanence of intimate relationships and about sexual identity and adequacy. Children of all ages are also uniquely able to blame themselves for their parents' divorces; they may display anger but feel depressed, guilty, shameful, and unlovable. Finally, more critical than when a divorce takes place is how it takes place. An angry, bitter, vengeful divorce at any developmental period is more damaging than one in which parents are supportive of each other's role as a parent and supportive of the children.

Preparing the Report

Short of actual testimony, which is the same in custody actions as in other types of cases and follows the guidelines in Chapter 18, the final step is writing the evaluation report. Chapter 17 discusses writing these reports and presents a sample outline for a custody evaluation report. As with all other reports presented to the courts, the custody evaluation should be free of jargon, the "psychobabble" comfortable for mental health professionals but meaningless to judges and attorneys. It should be straightforward and unambiguous; the bases for conclusions and recommendations must be clear.

Although the evaluation report is usually a major consideration in a custody action, it is not the only one, nor is it always the determining one. Therefore, the report should serve as an aid—to all parties, one hopes—to resolve the interpersonal problems that often extend far beyond the custody action itself. A report that recommends ways to resolve animosities, promote communication, and generally help those involved get on with their lives will be far more useful than one which simply recommends a child's custody or principal place of residence. The mental health professional is uniquely able to prepare such a report, and his or her observations can smooth the way for parents and children alike.

A Concluding Note

Custody battles sometimes continue for years after a divorce. One or both parents try to convert the child to his or her cause, to extend the divorce war by fighting over the child's loyalty. Sometimes these attempts are blatant: accusations of the other parent's ineptness or dangerousness, for example, can fly back and forth. Other attempts are subtle: silent but obvious "victim" acts, undue fear of the other parent, sabotaged contact between the child and the other parent. (See Clawar and Rivlin, 1991, and Gardner, 1986.) Most commonly these on-going struggles represent failure to resolve emotional issues between parents and to move on to the business of parenting, not continue to relate as ex-spouses. A parent fueling such a struggle would do well to regard the ex-spouse as the child's mother or father, not the enemy. Everyone benefits, not the least the child, for the child may view an attack on an ex-spouse as an attack on him or herself.

So-called "no fault" divorce and the emphasis on joint custody have tried to mitigate the acrimony and polarization so potentially corrosive after divorce. And, they seem to have helped. So have options to mediate rather than litigate and to subject disputes to arbitration outside of the courtroom. However, as noted before, divorcing grew up within an adversarial system and became an adversarial process although—and this is key—the principals usually have long-standing emotional ties. Unlike many other disputes that come before the courts, most divorces occur between people who, at least at some time, cared for each other. Not uncommonly, they still do. Yet the process of divorce requires them to go to war and results in the feelings of betrayal, anger, misunderstanding, threat, attack, and fright that so often occur.

There are no easy solutions to the problem of potential post-divorce psychological mayhem and its inevitable effects on children. However, before the situation gets substantially better, one thing, it seems, must occur. The public—those people who could someday themselves face divorce—must change their win-lose mindset about divorce. Attorneys are rarely rabble-rousers, responsible for the combat that ensues. They have jobs to do, and often a major part of those jobs is keeping a rein on the client who wants his or her pound of flesh. Rather, it is husbands and wives who must learn to approach divorce differently. They might regard it as a life passage and turn to their responsibilities as parents, handling them with the utmost care and collaboration even under difficult circumstances, negotiating in as businesslike a manner while protecting the children, not using them as pawns.

Can this happen? Perhaps. However, it will require education to change the perspectives of marrying and married people long before divorce comes up. Just as people who remain married find themselves alienated and alone if they argue to win rather than to communicate, so will divorcing people intent on conquest wind up embittered and feeling betrayed. Only by learning to regard divorce as an unfortunate but sometimes necessary outcome to marriage—not a battle to the death—can the situation change.

REFERENCES

APA Committee on Professional Practice and Standards' Development of Child Custody Guidelines, *APA Monitor,* 1992.

Clawar, S. and Rivlin, B. *Children Held Hostage: Dealing with Programmed and Brainwashed Children.* Chicago, IL: APA Psychology and Law Division, 1991.

Gardner, R. *Child Custody Litigation: A Guide for Parents and Mental Health Professionals.* Crestville, NJ: Creative Therapeutics, 1986.

Goldstein, J., Freud, A., and Solnit, A. *Beyond the Best Interest of the Child.* New York: The Free Press, 1973.

Gordon, R. and Peek, L. *The Custody Quotient.* Dallas: Wilmington Institute, 1987.

Kline, M., Tschann, J. M., Johnson, J. Z., and Wallerstein, J. "Childrens' Adjustment in Joint and Sole Custody Families," *Developmental Psychology,* No. 25, 430–438, 1989.

Roman, M. and Haddad, W. *The Disposable Parent.* New York: Holt, Reinhart, and Winston, 1978.

Uniform Marriage and Divorce Act, 402, 9A UCA (197–198), 1979.

Weithorn, L.A. (ed.) *Psychology and Child Custody Determinations.* Lincoln: University of Nebraska Press, 1987.

Chapter 13

MEDIATION AND OTHER OPTIONS TO LITIGATION

Many of us recall the wisdom attributed to Solomon in settling one of the earliest custody cases on record. In that case, each of two "mothers" claimed the same child as hers. King Solomon heard the dispute; he determined that the child should be cut in half and half given to each woman. Of course, the real mother, genuinely concerned for her child, immediately agreed to relinquish her claim rather than see the child killed to resolve the dispute. Solomon is rightly credited with the wisdom to foresee such an outcome, but the real mother was just as wise: compassionate, logical, and objective.

Parents involved in custody suits today have options short of cutting their children in half or, more significantly, having strangers—however wise—make decisions for them. Mediation and related processes are increasingly available in many states and even required in some. In such states, courts can ask mental health professionals and experts in other fields, such as attorneys, to help people resolve a variety of disputes outside the courtroom. While such services extend beyond courtroom testimony, they are discussed here because they naturally grow out of the role of the mental health professional in court.

The Job and Benefit of Mediation

In mediation, a neutral third party tries to help the principals construct a mutually satisfactory resolution to their disagreement. The mediator serves as a facilitator, looking for options, exploring alternatives, suggesting trade-offs, but never imposing solutions. Rather, the principals build their own.

Such an approach to resolving differences is theoretically sound. Ample research has shown that people who participate in problem-solving tend to live by the solutions better than those who have had solutions imposed on them. Two divorcing parents agreeing between themselves to a child contact schedule are more likely to view it as satisfactory and adhere to it than two parents forced to comply with a schedule that is identical but imposed by a judge.

Because mediation seeks solutions by parties' mutual agreement, not the intimidation or acquiescence of one to a distasteful outcome, the mediator must neutralize power as the mediation progresses. Still, some people can not take part in mediation, no matter how effective the mediator is. Some are simply too angry and hostile. Some, such as battered spouses, are in no position to make use of it. But others find mediation a sensible approach to resolving differences, particularly custody issues. Often the process of communicating and collaborating enhances both parties' skills, to everyone's benefit.

The Mediator

Various professionals may serve as mediators, including attorneys and mental health professionals. An attorney serving as mediator will probably bring a different perspective to the situation than a mental health professional. Sometimes the two collaborate. In a custody case, for example, the attorney might rely on the mental health professional for information about the child's emotional status, while the mental health professional would look to the attorney for information on legal requirements, limits, precedents, and so on. It is important to note that an attorney functioning as mediator is *not* functioning as advocate and cannot represent the parties as an attorney. The attorney acting as mediator plays a role much closer to that of the mental health professional, one of impartial assistant rather than advocate.

The Process of Mediation

Mediation begins by collecting basic data about the dispute. Then follows an introductory session to discuss the situation, general issues related to the dispute, and the general goal that will guide future sessions. In a custody case, the introductory session might try to reach agreement to do what's best for the child rather than determine a winning and losing parent. As sessions proceed, principals may disagree or polarize, and referring to this goal can help get discussions back on track.

The climate established in the introduction is critical to the success of mediation. Parties must be encouraged to be positive and open-minded, to seek solutions that meet the goal of the mediation and not just their personal objectives. Successful mediations proceed through the sessions required to reach such solutions. The mediator works to ensure not only that principals create mutually acceptable solutions but also that the solutions are realistic. For example, a custody mediation might result in a solution acceptable to the parents but insensitive to a child's needs. Then, the mediator should ask the principals to evaluate their solution in light of the goal of the mediation and help them work further on it to meet that goal.

Arbitration

When mediation is not possible or successful, disagreements may be settled by arbitration. Arbitration may be non-binding—the principals need not abide by the result—or binding. In either case, arbitration is more like litigation in that each principal presents his or her case to a neutral arbitrator. The arbitrator hears the arguments and proposes or imposes a solution. Despite its similarity to litigation, however, arbitration lacks the cues, the emotional triggers, to the polarization that often results from formal litigation. Simply having separate attorneys and going to court, with all the attendant motions, replies, depositions, and interrogations, can lock people into a battle stance. Avoiding these trappings sometimes avoids the hostility of battle as well.

Conciliation

Between arbitration and mediation is conciliation. Like mediation, a neutral third party tries to help the parties reach their own solution, but as in non-binding arbitration the third party offers suggestions, direction, and advice. The conciliator is neither strictly facilitator nor strictly decision-maker but a little of both.

A Proposal for Modified Conciliation

This chapter proposes a fourth model for use in custody disputes. That is a modified conciliation model in which the conciliator also acts as evaluator. The conciliator in a custody case would be a mental health professional who has evaluated the child or who has read the results of a custody evaluation so that conciliation serves not just the general or hypothetical best interests of any child but the particular and personal best interests of *this* child.

In such a case, the conciliator would know the child's psychological status, his or her needs, the nature of his or her relationships, his or her adaptability, and the potential impact on the child of various custody arrangements. The mediator would know, for example, that giving any child the responsibility for choosing one parent (and thereby rejecting the other) could be very damaging and would prevent parents from acting on such an agreement. Furthermore, the professional serving as conciliator in a modified conciliation would reject other solutions that might be damaging to *this* child, perhaps because of relationships with siblings or other unique conditions. The conciliator would help the parents understand why some solutions were potentially damaging and why other options might be preferred.

An actual case illustrates both the failings of traditional mediation and the process of modified conciliation. Although it is difficult to imagine, a mediator actually allowed parents disputing their child's custody to have the child decide which parent he wanted to live with—and not just at the time of the parents' divorce but again after several trial periods with the parent he had chosen first. The result was not difficult to imagine: a deeply troubled child. Effective mediation but certainly modified conciliation would have prevented parents from forcing their child to choose between them once, let alone more than once. However, modified conciliation would recognize that re-evaluating a custody agreement after a period of time might be a good idea in a particular case. If problems existed, they could be weighed against the problems that would arise from making a change. Under modified conciliation, such a recommendation would be based on its appropriateness and consequences in a given case, and it would be the responsibility of the parents, the conciliator, and the court, not the child.

The Benefits of Options to Litigation

Regardless of the method used to resolve custody disputes, the court retains jurisdiction over the child, and its jurisdiction can not and should not be pre-empted. Litigation is always the final resort. However, methods of resolution short of litigation have a number of advantages. First, the courts are clogged with domestic cases. In some jurisdictions, just getting a position on the docket is a major undertaking.

Second, the emotional costs of hostility arising in custody litigation and in the conflicts and returns to court commonly following divorce are enormous. Children are growing up frustrated, angry, confused, alienated, and caught between warring factions because of acrimonious battle that victimizes them again and again. Such children grow into adulthood mistrustful of relationships and mindful of potential emotional devastation, yet they are likely to create the same traps as have been laid for them, too often extending the legacy to still another generation. Indeed, it would seem that the plight of children of divorce in this country is a significant public health problem not resolvable by the court or legal system alone.

Options to litigation remove disputes from the win—lose, adversarial arena that is, by definition, the court. In custody matters, modified conciliation gives parents the opportunity to forge arrangements that will work both physically and emotionally for themselves and their child after divorce. Options to litigation give disagreeing parents—and parties to other disputes—the chance to be as wise as the real mother in the tale of King Solomon.

REFERENCES

Coogler, O. *Structured Mediation in Divorce Settlement: A Handbook for Marital Mediation.* New York: Lexington Books, 1978.

Folberg, J. and Taylor, A. *Mediation: A Comprehensive Guide to Resolving Conflicts without Litigation.* San Francisco: Josey-Bass, 1984.

Haynes, J. *Divorce Mediation: A Practical Guide for Therapists and Counselors.* New York: Springer, 1981.

Kressel, K., Lopez-Marillas, M., Weingass, J., and Deutsch, M. *Professional Intervention in Divorce: the Views of the Lawyers, Therapists, and Clergy.* In Levinger, G. and Moles, O., eds., *Divorce and Separation.* New York: Basic Books, 1979.

Chapter 14

PERSONAL INJURY CASES

Mental health professionals are often called into personal injury cases to assess emotional or other consequences of untoward events. Personal injury cases are one type of tort, or case stemming from a breach of duty. A tort is a civil violation of case law or common law, the body of law based on judicial decisions, principally in England, derived from custom and precedent, and forming a body of "unwritten law."

Elements of a Tort

A tort has several elements. First, there must be some kind of legal obligation from the defendant to the plaintiff, usually not a formal obligation by contract but a duty arising from circumstances. For example, an individual owning a vicious dog has an unwritten obligation to maintain control over the animal; failure to do so would be considered a breach of implicit duty.

Such a breach constitutes the second element of a tort. If the owner of the vicious dog allows the dog to roam the neighborhood, whether through carelessness, neglect, or intent, the owner has clearly breached his or her duty to protect others from the dog.

The third element of the tort is the existence of compensible damage resulting from the breach. A vicious dog crossing the neighbor's lawn only to sniff a tree and return home would likely not qualify. The custom of compensating people for wrongs or injuries has historical roots extending back many centuries. In torts, victims may be compensated for pain and suffering, lost wages, or some other demonstrable loss.

The fourth element, a critical one, is that the breach of duty is the "proximate cause" of the injury or damage. The defendant's breach of duty must have produced the plaintiff's injury; without the breach, the injury would not have occurred.

In addition to breach of duty, a tort—then called a "derivative tort"—can arise out of criminal activity. For example, a person "traumatized" in a robbery may seek civil remedy independent of any criminal prosecution arising from the crime itself.

Cases of Mental Trauma

Several types of personal injury cases can involve the services of mental health professionals. In the most common, mental "trauma," sometimes called "traumatic neurosis" or "post-traumatic stress disorder," results from an injury. Because of the injurious event, the plaintiff may suffer emotional distress exhibited in a wide range of symptoms. For example, an individual involved in a car wreck may incur an acute anxiety while driving or even a phobia for being in an automobile. The most severe post-traumatic stress disorders can result in emotional consequences so debilitating that their sufferers are dysfunctional. The emotional reactions of some soldiers to experiences in Vietnam—some resulting in psychosis or violent behavior—demonstrate the destructive potential of mental trauma.

Because at issue is breach of duty resulting in a compensible injury to the plaintiff, one of the mental health professional's most important diagnostic tools is a detailed history of the plaintiff's functioning prior to the event. Others' observations, records of previous treatment, and previous test data will help establish a "base line" describing the plaintiff's functioning prior to the alleged cause of present injuries. The absence of "base line" information may cloud the picture considerably, particularly in cases of post-traumatic stress disorder. Tests of the victim's current state may provide valuable information, but the disorder is by definition debilitating change over time. So, while tests or other techniques may determine that an individual is anxious, depressed, or phobic now, they may not be able to reach back in time and establish definitively that the alleged breach of duty was the proximate cause of current symptoms. Therefore, just as in all other forensic assessments, the expert must examine all available data carefully to arrive at sound, unbiased opinions.

Other Injury Cases

Mental distress is not the only basis for involving mental health professionals in personal injury cases. Other cases include head injuries and disfiguring or debilitating physical injuries. In head injury cases, the mental health professional may administer neuropsychological tests. These tests help to diagnose an individual's condition by assessing correlates of brain damage to determine the individual's losses and capabilities. Highly sophisticated medical techniques such as CAT (computerized axial tomography) scanning and MRI (magnetic resonance imagery) have diminished the importance of neuropsychological testing in diagnosing brain tissue damage. Nonetheless, neuropsychological testing can assess behavioral strengths and limitations caused by head injury fairly precisely. A neuropsychologist may also be able to make prognoses about the individual's future. Both assessing damage and making prognoses are important elements in personal injury cases.

Other physical injuries may warrant a mental health professional's opinion about the victim's "body image" and its relationship to interpersonal functioning and self esteem. For example, consider the case of an attractive teen-age girl who is badly burned and whose legs remain severely scarred. The scars will most likely affect her perception of her own attractiveness and limit the way she dresses all of her life. Physical injury may also alter an individual's confidence and sense of worth, affecting his or her performance on the job. An actor whose face is his "fortune" may suffer inestimably from disfigurement. A salesman who incurs a visible physical injury may find his career path destroyed. So too may deliterious effects of occupational stress be tortious if a breach of duty is the proximate cause.

Just as some who incur debilitating injuries are decimated by them, others take them well in stride. While the mental health professional may not be able to predict how a given individual will react to a future injury, understanding the individual's vulnerability is an important part of a personal injury assessment. By the same token, many who show significant emotional distress after an injury showed no signs of disturbance before the injury, while others had obvious and documented problems all along. Consider, for example, an individual in treatment for severe anxiety. The individual is involved in an automobile accident. Afterward, she develops a phobia of driving, aggravation and intensification of the original anxiety attacks, and other emotional dysfunctions far more severe than before.

Taking Victims as They Are

In the eyes of the law, personal injury victims' prior problems do not diminish problems resulting from the injury. One convention of law says in effect that we must take our victims as we find them. To cite a homely analogy, if we crash into a truck carrying eggs and break them all, we can not claim that the truck should have been loaded with golf balls. By extension, it makes no difference that we rear-end a car whose driver already had significant back and neck problems and that the victim is more vulnerable to the effects of the crash than someone with a healthy spine. Just as the law does not, mental health professionals must not fail to consider a victim's pre-existing conditions in assessing the effects of personal injury.

The Importance of Mental Health Testimony

Given that a plaintiff has been involved in some event that proximately causes symptoms or handicaps, one might ask whether the mental health professional's examination is superfluous. If the plaintiff is capable of explaining the nature and extent of the injuries, why call in an expert? There are several reasons.

First, the mental health professional lends credence to the victim's complaints. Forensic evaluations almost always assess malingering, and personal injury cases hold special potential for fraud. The mental health professional is called on to validate (or invalidate) the plaintiff's complaints objectively. In so doing, the mental health professional counteracts any impression the plaintiff might otherwise make as a whiner or moaner should he or she take the stand alone to recite a litany of complaints. The mental health expert also helps jurors understand injuries they can not "see." The expert can help the jury distinguish between previous conditions, should they exist, and current conditions resulting from the injury. Knowing how conditions relate to each other helps the jury appreciate the nature and extent of new symptoms rather than dismiss them as simply more of what had been there for years.

Most important, however, the mental health professional can help prevent jurors from projecting their own feelings onto the victim. A juror who could never imagine suffering phobia of driving after an auto accident might regard a victim who does as faking or weak. The expert witness must clearly explain the mechanisms—the psychic vulnerabilities—by which the victim's phobic symptoms developed and how those mechanisms are different for the plaintiff than they may be for others. Such an explanation helps jurors to shed their own preconceptions of how "all people" are or should be and gain greater empathy for the plaintiff's plight (Harrison, 1990).

In telling the victim's unique story, the expert witness may also be able to explain the subjective reality to which the plaintiff is responding rather than a more objective and sterile interpretation of the precipitating event. People respond to their subjective realities, especially in crises, and may misperceive as dangerous situations which when viewed objectively are simply not. A store clerk "held up" at the point of a squirt gun by a kid playing a joke may genuinely believe that his life is in danger even though he later sees that the weapon is obviously a toy. If he had previously been robbed at gunpoint, his misperception may be even more understandable. This phenomenon is particularly important in clinical diagnoses of post-traumatic stress disorder. The American Psychiatric Association's *Diagnostic and Statistical Manual* defines the stressors that produce such trauma as "outside the range of usual human experience and markedly distressing to almost anyone, e.g., serious threat to one's life or physical integrity; serious threat or harm to one's children, spouse, or other close relatives and friends; sudden destruction of one's home or community; or seeing another person who has recently been or is being seriously injured or killed as a result of an accident or physical violence." (DSM–III–R, 1987, p. 250.) Mental health testimony should explain such stresses—and the victim's responses—to a jury in terms jurors can understand even if they have not experienced similar stresses themselves.

Psychological disorders are usually invisible. A plaintiff in a wheelchair presents a far different picture to the jury than one who is inwardly tormented. The mental health professional can validate that torment and explain to the jury how the plaintiff came to this end—or unmask the malingerer seeking a financial "kill."

REFERENCES

American Psychiatric Association. *Diagnostic and Statistical Manual of Mental Disorders,* Third Edition. Washington, DC: American Psychiatric Association, 1987.

Harrison, T.F. "How to Win an Emotional Distress Case." *Lawyers' Alert,* Vol. 10, No. 4, 1990.

Homant, Robert J. "Assessing Psychological Damages of Crime Victims." *Trial,* 1989, pgs. 86–90.

Chapter 15

CIVIL COMPETENCE AND COMMITMENT

The judicial system uses the term "competence" in both civil and criminal contexts. However, it has vastly different meanings. In criminal cases, "competence" describes one's ability to stand trial (see Chapter 7). In civil matters, "competence" describes one's ability to manage one's affairs and to act autonomously.

The ability to manage one's affairs is usually tied closely to the ability to manage money in everyday situations. Competent individuals know the relative values of monetary denominations, count change, and have awareness—however crude—of checking and savings accounts, loans, and taxes. Individuals who act autonomously are not unduly susceptible to the influence of others. They need not be very sophisticated, and they may be vulnerable to con artists who are, but they do not automatically fall prey to deception at the hands of unscrupulous friends and relatives trying to bilk them.

The latter aspect of competence may seem shocking. However, greed can have extreme effects, even on people who were previously trustworthy. One case illustrates such effects. A fairly wealthy man was hospitalized and on life support equipment to treat an illness that was neither terminal nor life-threatening. Nonetheless, his children, their eyes on their inheritance, asked that "the plug be pulled." In other less dramatic instances, funds and assets are slowly siphoned away or "borrowed" from unsuspecting individuals. At both extremes, the victims need protection. They do not, however, necessarily require confinement or hospitalization.

Declaring Incompetence

Having a person declared in need of a guardian or conservator involves a legal process to ensure the person's rights. The process varies from state to state, but in all cases it is formal and can not be accomplished out-of-hand by someone who stands to gain by the result. In some states, a petition is filed with the Probate Court; the person alleged to be incompetent is notified and an examination takes place. Prior to the hearing, the court may appoint an attorney to represent the person. At the hearing, the court hears evidence of the person's ability to make evaluations and decisions to manage his or her affairs and meet his or her needs for physical health and safety.

State laws governing civil competence vary widely and often lack clear guidelines for its determination. The court may find the individual fully competent, fully incompetent, or, in some states, of limited competence (Melton, 1987). That is, the person's decision-making autonomy may be restricted but not eliminated. For example, a person owning and managing a complicated business might be required to relinquish its control but might be allowed to continue to handle personal or circumscribed financial transactions.

However, once an individual is judged incompetent, the states fairly consistently appoint a guardian or conservator to manage all or some of the individual's affairs. Guardian- or conservatorship does not give *carte blanche* to do what one wants; the guardian is expected to act responsibly and can be held legally accountable for failing to do so.

Determining competence is, of course, the job of the judge, not a mental health professional. Nor is a mental health diagnosis necessarily relevant. A person labeled "schizophrenic" need not be incompetent to manage his or her affairs, and a person diagnosed as mentally retarded may still be able to remain independent. So, the mental health professional can best serve the court by assessing the individual's ability to function in a range of situations. What the individual can and cannot reasonably be expected to *do* is far more important than any diagnostic label.

Evaluating Civil Competence

The competency evaluation, then, should examine the person's cognitive functioning—not just "I.Q.," but intellectual and adaptive functioning in the broadest sense. The evaluation should also assess the individual's emotional status, its potential chronicity, and its amenability to treatment. The mental health professional should keep in mind the possible limitations to the individual's functioning and the possible need for a guardian, not simply a diagnosis.

To these ends, the evaluator should obtain a detailed history from the subject, corollary sources, or documents to establish performance in relevant situations. Psychological tests can assess intellect, but the evaluator should also look for the ability to reason, make judgments, remember, concentrate, calculate, be aware of time, place, and other people, and have insight into situations. I.Q. alone is likely to be relevant only if it is so low that one doesn't really need a test to measure it. Other cognitive factors to assess are the presence or absence of delusions, hallucinations, and formal thought disorders as they affect the person's ability to manage his or her affairs. Some "crazy" people do quite well in the everyday world, pointing up the importance of legal and functional criteria for competence, not just psychiatric ones.

The evaluator should also assess general personality make-up, emotional variables such as depression, anxiety, phobia, mania, substance dependence, and the interaction of emotional and cognitive variables. The importance of examining the interaction of variables is demonstrated by a condition sometimes called "pseudo-dementia." In one case, an individual was committed as incompetent and in need of constant nursing home care. The mental health professional evaluating the patient found him virtually unresponsive and largely unaware of the goings-on around him. He could, in fact, not function without constant care and supervision. His debility was believed to have been the result of an accidental closed head injury. However, the evaluator found the severity of the symptoms to extend far beyond those attributable to the injury. The patient was diagnosed as suffering, in part, from pseudo-dementia, a condition of the mind complicated by a major depressive overlay. The patient was treated aggressively with antidepressant medications and shortly became alert and responsive. Some brain dysfunction remained from the accident, but it was not severe enough, once the depression was eliminated, to warrant the kind of care initially required.

Such interactions of depression with, for example, relatively mild cognitive loss brought about by stroke, early Alzheimer's disease, or other medical conditions, may well cause an inability to manage one's affairs or even take care of oneself. However, treating the depression may quickly restore the person to a much higher level of functioning, as this example illustrates. Sometimes simply over-medication brought on by the reasoning that "if one is good, two (or more) are better" can produce "incompetence" that should not really exist—and may be easily changed. Here one might look for a pattern of deterioration which may correlate with attempts to remediate some particular condition.

Competence and Commitment

Although they are not necessarily linked, needs for civil commitment sometimes accompany incompetence to manage one's affairs; one may be so incompetent as to constitute a danger to oneself, as patients in late stages of Alzheimer's disease may be. As with competence, states' criteria for deciding on commitment vary. However, they generally ride on the belief that, because of mental illness, an individual presents a clear and imminent or present danger to him or herself or others. Danger to oneself is more common in civil issues—for example, the risk of suicide—than danger to others. The words "imminent" and "present" are important: the individual must be dangerous now or very shortly, not two years from now. In emergencies, individuals may be held temporarily, usually for 48 to 72 hours, to assess the need for longer-term commitment. Even then, the need for continued commitment must be periodically reviewed.

Some jurisdictions recognize a third basis for commitment, and that is whether the individual can make critical judgments in conducting his or her life. Under such a criterion, an individual who lacks the ability to recognize the need for treatment, even though behavior places him or her at risk, may be committed. Severe alcoholics may thus be found incapable of making appropriate judgments and held for treatment or at least detoxification.

Contrary to some popular beliefs, mental health professionals have no power to commit people involuntarily to hospitals. This right is reserved to the courts through various petitioners, usually next of kin. However, police officers and mental health professionals may request civil commitment, and ultimately a mental health assessment would take place to determine if such a commitment is in fact warranted on psychological or psychiatric grounds.

Furthermore, no longer can people be committed and "put away forever," even though some believe they can. Wyatt vs. Stickney (1971) affirmed the right to adequate treatment so that no longer could people be "warehoused." Lake vs. Cameron (1966) further required that individuals must be committed in the "least restrictive environment." (See U. S. vs. Brawner, 1972.) Addington vs. Texas (1978) established that "clear and convincing evidence" was required to prove the need for commitment. These legal protections guard against the abusive and involuntary lockups in years past.

However, there are unfortunate consequences to easing the limits of custodial care, and one is the rise in the homeless population. Many who live on the street are mentally ill but not dangerous, and so the state cannot hold them. Because the homeless mentally ill often lack the resources and abilities to function well in society, they remain at the fringe, often in pain and despair, and a source of shame for one of the wealthiest nations on earth. On the other hand, to require commitment is to deprive them of their individual liberties and fundamental constitutional rights.

Clearly, the issues of competence and commitment are important, since an individual may lose all or part of his or her autonomy. Aiding the court through a thorough evaluation is another important contributions the mental health professional can make to the court—and to the individuals involved.

REFERENCES

Addington vs. Texas, 441 U. S. 418, 428 (1978).
Lake vs. Cameron, 364 F. 2d 657, DC Cir., (1966).
Melton, G. B., Petrila, V., Poythress, N. G., and Slobogin, C. *Psychological Evaluations for the Courts.* New York: The Guilford Press, 1987.
U. S. vs. Brawner, 471 F. 2d 969, DC Cir., (1972).
Wyatt vs. Stickney, 325 F. Supp. 781, Alabama (1971).

Chapter 16

PSYCHOLOGICAL RECONSTRUCTION

In the 1950s and 1960s, psychologists including Edwin Schneidman began intensely studying suicide and self-destructive behavior (Schneidman and Faberow, 1957). Schneidman coined the term "suicidology" to describe their work, which attempted not only to gain insight into the prevention and treatment of suicide but also to resolve "undetermined" causes of death.

Many unnatural causes of death—suicide, homicide, and accident—go undetected because of lack of suspicion, interest, care, or adequate knowledge and training (Jobes and Josselson, 1987). Sometimes, medical pathology does not determine a certain cause of death, leaving it to speculation. Suicide victims have been known to try to disguise their acts, perhaps so survivors can collect insurance, just as some killers try to make their deeds look like accidents.

The Psychological Autopsy

As part of a much larger field of investigation, Schneidman advocated a multidisciplinary approach to investigating deaths with undetermined causes. Out of this work came the "psychological autopsy" (Schneidman, 1976), a supplement to the medical autopsy in equivocal or suspicious cases. As Wekstein (1979) notes, seemingly irrelevant data such as occupation, family history, marital status, religious preference, and hobbies can provide information critical to establishing the cause of death. An outline for the psychological autopsy appears in Schneidman (1976).

Further criteria for investigating suicide appear in Jobes and Josselson (1987). Direct intent may be validated by witnesses to verbal expressions or non-verbal behavior showing serious depression or response to loss or stress. Other clues may also help, among them unexpected or inappropriate but unmistakable preparations for death, such as putting affairs in order and settling accounts, expressions of hopelessness, inquiries about means of death, farewells to others, and so on. Investigators should also consider prior suicide attempts or threats, the presence or absence of support systems, debilitating illness, easy access to effective means of suicide, and non-flamboyant or manipulative suicide notes (Meyer et al., 1988). One particularly ominous sign is the sudden and inexplicable improvement in mood in a very depressed person. Often this signals relief at having decided to commit suicide.

Reconstructing a Descedant's State of Mind

The term "psychological autopsy" has largely been replaced by the term "reconstruction." Its techniques apply today not only to investigating suicide but also to assessing, for example, a descedant's state of mind at the time of executing a will. Wills begin with the words, "being of sound mind," or an equivalent expression of mental capacity required to make the will valid. But wills are sometimes contested by survivors who claim the descedant was not of sound mind at the time the will was drawn. Being of sound mind requires knowledge, at least generally, of the nature and extent of one's property, those who may lay claim to it, and how the will will distribute it. Mental illness, substance abuse, or other potentially mitigating conditions need not preclude drawing a valid will as long as the will was constructed during a "lucid interval" (Melton, 1987).

Mental health professionals may be called on to reconstruct a descedant's mental state at the time a will was drawn. The reconstruction evaluates functional capacity—the effectiveness of the individual's adaptive behavior and understanding—just as an evaluation of civil competence does; the only difference is that in reconstruction, the mental health expert must gather sufficient information to assess competence in an earlier time and without examining the subject.

Consider, for example, a situation in which a wealthy widower, lonely, depressed, despondent, and described as having had short periods of confusion, memory loss, and disorientation, signs a new will leaving his entire estate to the woman he marries later the same day. Suspicious? Yes, of course, but if that's what the widower wanted to do, he had every right to do it as long as he was of sound mind at the time and not under undue, irresistable influence.

If such a will is challenged, the information the clinician seeks about the descedant's state of mind adds up to a conclusion of "soundness" or "unsoundness." One might be suspicious of pseudo-dementia, possible transient ischemic episodes, passivity and depression in the face of undue pressure or manipulation, and a host of similar variables. These are assessed by interviewing those close to the subject at the time in question and reviewing letters and other documents written by the subject during that time. As in assessing civil competence, the mental health professional must be as sensitive to the motivations of interviewees as to the evidence they present.

The court uses the mental health expert's conclusion to decide whether the will has probative value, or validity. If the court finds the will to have no probative value, it admits a prior will if one exists. If no prior will exists, the subject is found to have died intestate and assets are distributed according to the probate laws of the state. In some cases, knowing the terms of a prior will or how the assets of intestate individuals are divided will help the clinician fully assess survivors' motivations to contest a will.

Psychological Profiling

Psychological reconstruction also helps to investigate and analyze crime scenes. Commonly known as "profiling" or crime scene analysis, the methodology evolved from work by the Federal Bureau of Investigation's Behavioral Sciences Unit as a tool for trained law enforcement personnel. It became famous in hunts for serial killers and was featured in the 1991 Academy Award-winning movie, *The Silence of the Lambs.*

Profiling takes an actuarial or statistical approach to analyzing psychological data; it researches correlates of pieces of information surrounding a crime, and if they are found to be statistically reliable and valid, uses them to make probability statements about the criminal's personality, habits, motives, and so on. Profiling is most productive in crimes in which the unknown suspect has shown significant psychopathology—for example, sadistic torture, apparently motiveless arson, mutilation, ritualistic crimes, and often rapes (Geberth, 1981).

Sexual murderers, for example, have been shown to see their world as unjust, devalue the victim and society at large, be preoccupied with dominance achieved by aggression and often confuse fantasy and reality (FBI, 1985). Rape also has strong elements of needs to control either verbally or with physical force. Analyzing how and why crimes are committed as well as criminals' other verbal, sexual, and physical behavior may help law enforcement personnel understand criminals' personality characteristics and needs. Then, they can better predict their patterns of behavior and, when suspects' patterns match up, contribute to the solution of crimes.

REFERENCES

Federal Bureau of Investigation. "The Men Who Murdered," *FBI Law Enforcement Bulletin,* Vol. 54, No. 8, 1985.

Geberth, V. "Psychological Profiling," *Law and Order,* September, 1981.

Gist, R. Personal communication, January, 1992.

Jobes, D. and Josselson, A. "Improving the Validity and Reliability of Medical–Legal Certifications of Suicide," *Suicide and Life Threatening Behavior,* Vol. 17, Winter, 1987.

Melton, G. B., Petrila, J., Poythress, N. G., and Slobogin, C. *Psychological Evaluations for the Courts.* New York: The Guilford Press, 1987.

Meyer, R., Landis, E., and Hays, J. *Law for the Psychotherapist.* New York: W. W. Norton, 1988.

Schneidman, E., ed. *Suicidology: Contemporary Developments.* New York: Green and Stratton, 1976.

Schneidman, E. and Faberow, N. "Some Comparisons Between Genuine and Simulated Suicide Notes." *Journal of General Psychology,* Vol. 56, 1957.

Wekstein, L. *Handbook of Suicidology: Principles, Problems, and Practices.* New York: Bruner-Mazel, 1979.

Section IV
AFTER THE EVALUATION

Chapter 17

PREPARING THE EVALUATION REPORT

Forensic evaluation reports are similar to other clinical evaluation reports, and the mental health professional follows similar steps in preparing them. All types of evaluations are basically detective work in which the clinician attempts to build a picture of an individual from information gained piece by piece, just as a mosaic is built tile by tile. For example, seeing a spent shell casing in a parking lot would lead one to hypothesize, within reasonable limits of probability, that a bullet had been fired. We do not have enough information, however, to determine whether it was fired in the parking lot or at another location, in the context of a crime or not, and whether it caused an injury. We need much more information to build the mosaic depicting what happened. So it is with psychological assessment. Each interview, each instrument should add something to the overall picture. Each addition must be interpreted along with all other pertinent information to lead to sound conclusions.

However, the objectives of a forensic evaluation report are different from the objectives of other evaluation reports. Rather than just concluding with a diagnosis or treatment plan, the forensic evaluation report relates results to legal criteria. In fact, diagnoses sometimes have no place in a forensic evaluation report, although treatment plans may be relevant. As the DSM III–R puts it, "The clinical and scientific considerations involved in categorization of these conditions as mental disorders may not be wholly relevant to legal judgments" (1989, p. xxix). In other words, the mental health professional must provide an opinion that meets legal, not just psychological or psychiatric criteria.

As an example, consider the M'Naghten rule for determining insanity discussed in Chapter 1. It holds that individuals are not criminally responsible if, because of mental disease or defect, they do not know the nature and quality of their acts or they do not know that what they are doing is wrong. In this case, determining that an individual suffers a mental disease or defect—reaching a diagnosis—is part of the clinician's work, but the diagnosis is far from all of it. The clinician must further attempt to connect the disease or defect to the individual's lack of knowledge about the nature and quality of an act or the inability to distinguish right from wrong at the time of the crime.

To illustrate, imagine a person who falsely believes that others are trying to poison him or, in clinical terms, is delusional. The individual commits a crime. The clinician must connect the person's delusional system to his lack of knowledge of right from wrong to support the use of the M'Naghten rule. In fact, the person may fully understand the nature and quality of his crime and know that it was wrong in spite of his delusion about being poisoned. As another example, the Battered Spouse syndrome—support for a defense of delayed self-defense in some states—nvolves an individual's mental state and perceptions at the time of a crime. Like the M'Naghten rule, it requires the clinician to link post-raumatic stress disorder as described in the DSM III–R to the commission of a crime, not just diagnose the disorder.

Collecting, Evaluating, and Interpreting the Data

As discussed earlier, the first phase of an evaluation is the collection of data. The clinical portion of this phase involves interviews and possibly a battery of psychological tests. Other portions may include reviewing a wide range of records such as earlier evaluations, police reports, depositions, school records, and so on.

The second phase is evaluating and interpreting the data. How does it all fit together, and what does it mean? How does it relate to the legal issues of the case? What conclusions and opinions does it support?

Reporting the Results

Third, the conclusions and bases for them must be effectively communicated, most often in a written report. The report constitutes official documentation of the mental health expert's activities and conclusions. The report will also be read by those who are not mental health professionals, and it may be subject to close inspection and potential dissection during cross-examination. It must therefore be clear, factual, relevant, and readable. Speculations should be clearly labeled and conclusions and opinions clearly supported. And, as in testimony, the expert must avoid jargon and psychobabble.

There are no rules for organizing the forensic evaluation report, and each author will have his or her own style. However, this chapter presents two annotated outlines that have worked in a variety of cases. The first is a general outline suitable in a wide range of situations. The second serves the often complex report of a custody evaluation.

General Forensic Evaluation Report

I. Administrative and Identifying Data

This section presents the name and age of the person evaluated, the date(s) of the evaluation, and the date of the report.

II. Referral Information

This section states the issues at hand and briefly describes the circumstances surrounding them. It also explains how the case came to be presented for evaluation.

III. Procedures

This section describes how the evaluation was conducted: who was interviewed, what tests were used, and what other documentation was reviewed.

IV. History

This section briefly summarizes relevant historical information about the subject of the evaluation and describes the events leading to the cause of the evaluation.

V. Results

This section presents the expert's findings. It summarizes interview, test, and any other data. It interprets the data to describe the subject's behavior, mental state, and general psychological make-up. Most effective reports integrate data to describe a particular person rather than simply presenting the data test by test or interview by interview; the latter approach can be discordant and redundant. However, that approach can work if it includes a summary that integrates and interprets the data.

VI. Discussion

This section is optional but may be useful to describe the issues in the case, how they relate to each other and the data at hand, alternative considerations, speculations—if they are relevant, and whatever else might help the reader understand the "big picture."

VI. Conclusions and Recommendations

This section presents final conclusions and recommendations. It ties results to the issues of the case; it answers the ultimate question, "So what?" The expert must take care not to form conclusions of law, which are the province of the court; this section should describe the subject's mental state at the time of the crime but should not conclude, for example, that the subject was insane. The expert may make recommendations, and these may be presented as a set of alternatives. For example, the expert might recommend inpatient treatment, but outpatient treatment and close supervision during probation might also be acceptable. Throughout, the report should present the bases for the conclusions and recommendations—the reasoning that led to them—so that the reader is not surprised by them but understands how they were reached.

VII. Summary

This brief section presents an overview of the entire report. It is similar to an abstract in a research report.

Custody Evaluation Report

The custody evaluation report tends to be more complex than other forensic evaluation reports. In part, its issues can be more complicated, but it also reports on the evaluation of more than one person and the interactions among them. The following outline shows that some sections are the same as in the general evaluation report while others are different.

I. Administrative and Identifying Data

This section presents the name and age of the people evaluated, the date(s) of the evaluation, and the date of the report.

II. Referral Information

This section states the issues at hand and briefly describes the circumstances surrounding them. It also explains how the case came to be presented for evaluation.

III. Procedures

This section describes how the evaluation was conducted: who was interviewed, what tests were used, and what other documentation was reviewed.

IV. History

This section briefly summarizes relevant historical information about the subjects of the evaluation and describes the events leading to the need for evaluation. In addition, it may recount allegations and positions of each of the parties and their subjective bases for these contentions. It describes the current child contact arrangement, each parent's role and the reasons for it, and each parent's understanding of the other parent's role.

It may also include collateral contacts or interviews if they shed light on the situation and information about the child's preferences. It is best never to ask a child directly which parent he or she prefers to live with, for that puts the child squarely in the middle of the dispute and aggravates an already stressful situation. A child "picking" a parent is then rejecting the other, in most cases a very difficult and guilt-inducing act. However, sometimes a child volunteers that information, and if that occurs, it may be included here. This section might also include information from a home study if one was done.

V. Results

This section presents the expert's findings. It summarizes interview, test, and any other data. It interprets the data to describe the subjects' behaviors, mental states, and general psychological make-ups. This section might be organized according to the parties involved and their interactions: data pertaining to the mother, then the father, then the child or children, and then relationships among them.

VI. Discussion

This section describes the issues in the case, how they relate to each other and the data at hand, alternative considerations, speculations—if they are relevant—and whatever else might help the reader understand the "big picture." It may also address the veracity of the spouses' allegations about each other. If one says the other is, for example, mentally ill, does that square with the evaluation results? If not, what might the allegation mean? If the child expressed a preference for living with one parent, the expert should interpret and explain that preference here (and not just take it at face value).

VII. Conclusions and Recommendations

This section presents final conclusions and recommendations, with alternatives, if appropriate. As with other evaluations, the mental health professional should make recommendations from a psychological or psychiatric perspective, but it is up to the court to review all the data and rule accordingly. Often the custody recommendation *per se* is the least important aspect of this section, while recommendations to end the conflict and resolve painful emotional issues are far more critical. This section should present the bases for the conclusions and recommendations—the lines of reasoning that led to them.

VIII. Summary

This brief section presents an overview of the entire report. It is similar to an abstract in a research report.

One of the most difficult aspects of a custody evaluation is including enough data to support conclusions and recommendations without inflaming the controversy or putting the child at risk. Sometimes, a child's statements "spill the beans" about a parent and open the child to retaliation. Excluding those statements can water down, even demolish, the bases for conclusions and recommendations. Telling the child that there won't be any secrets up front may be the only option, but that seems of little solace, and it may prevent the child from speaking his or her mind. Sometimes it is possible to have the court limit access to the report or portions of it to the parties' attorneys. If it is not possible, the evaluator should discuss possible consequences with the attorney who retained him or her to minimize possible damage.

The Value of the Report

To sum up, the evaluation report presents the expert's "evidence"—interview, test, and other data evaluated in the context of history and circumstances. Conclusions the mental health professional derives from these sources are offered to assist the court in reaching a just verdict more effectively than it could without such conclusions. The expert is to provide valid, reliable, and relevant information which goes beyond the information the average person could supply, but to present it in a form that the average person can understand.

REFERENCE

American Psychiatric Association. *Diagnostic and Statistical Manual of Mental Disorders.* Third Edition. Washington, DC: American Psychiatric Association, 1987.

Chapter 18

DELIVERING EFFECTIVE EXPERT TESTIMONY

As the previous chapters suggest, serving as an expert witness involves far more than speaking one's mind in court. As with so many other tasks, qualification and preparation are essential; preparation invariably takes the most time and effort. For these reasons, this chapter first reviews information presented elsewhere about qualifying and preparing to deliver expert testimony; then the expert takes the stand.

Qualification

The expert witness is expected to be exactly that, an expert on the matters at hand in a particular case. The mental health professional whose expertise is restricted to child psychology probably has no business testifying in an adult personal injury case. So, before agreeing to serve as an expert witness, the mental health professional should confer with counsel and learn enough about the case to determine that he or she is expert in the matters involved—and decline to serve if not. As we will discuss, the witness's qualifications come under close scrutiny before the first word of testimony is spoken, and an expert shown not to be so expert will embarrass client, counsel and self.

Preparation

During the first conferences with counsel, the expert witness should also begin preparation by discussing how a psychological evaluation can or cannot address the issues at hand. For example, a mental health professional called on to perform an evaluation in a custody dispute but denied access to both parents should point out the severe limitations he or she will face. The result will not be a "custody evaluation" recommending a particular arrangement. It can only conclude that the parent evaluated might or might not be an effective custodial parent.

Likewise, evaluating someone accused of sexually abusing a family member will probably yield only very limited data. Sex abusers fit no exclusive profile, and interviewing them alone rarely results in conclusions that support their guilt or innocence of alleged crimes.

The next step is the evaluation itself, which must be comprehensive, focused, and consistent with acceptable standards of practice. Other chapters in this book discuss unique considerations in various types of evaluations, for example in custody or personal injury cases. However, a general rule of thumb applies. The mental health professional should base primary conclusions from an evaluation on at least two significant sources of data and resolve any contradictions that may arise. Rarely will all information point in the same direction, and at times the clinician must form an opinion "on balance," much as the legal system looks for a "preponderance of evidence." Nevertheless, the clinician must account for contradictory data and, at the least, explain how and why it did or did not figure into his or her conclusions. Consider an example of a custody dispute. Parent A may show a range of strengths over Parent B but be a poor disciplinarian. The clinician may decide to recommend some kind of parenting instruction to overcome this weakness while still recommending that Parent A be the custodial parent.

Testing One's Conclusions

After completing an evaluation, organizing information, and drawing conclusions in an objective, impartial fashion, some expert witnesses find it useful to re-examine the data from an opposite point of view. In discussing custody evaluations, we presented an example of assuming the role of "devil's advocate." Doing so not only illuminates the strengths and weaknesses of the data and points out contradictions or lack of information but also makes good preparation for cross-examination. After all, arguing the position of a devil's advocate is exactly what opposing counsel will do with the expert's testimony.

Preparing for Effective Testimony

At this point, and if appropriate, the expert witness might discuss findings with the attorney and explore the kinds of questions to be asked in court which will best elicit the expert's opinion to the finders of fact. Would a graphic, for example, of an MMPI profile be helpful to the jury? Would it be better in this case to ask the expert's conclusions first and then their bases rather than begin with "What did such-and-such test tell you?" The expert should help the attorney understand how the expert's findings will address salient legal issues. The attorney will gain a greater understanding of the expert's contributions to the case and will be better able to fit the expert's testimony into the trial strategy. Understanding that strategy will help the expert complete preparations and testify effectively as well.

Testifying in court is, at least in one sense, a fairly straightforward set of operations. The commonly invoked "witness rule" requires that a witness not listen to other testimony before he or she testifies, so the witness waits outside the courtroom until called.

Establishing Expertise

After the witness is sworn in, he or she is first questioned to establish expertise. The expert witness need not have strings of degrees to qualify as "expert"; an expert witness is an individual regarded by the *court* as having specialized knowledge that will help the trier of fact decide the issues at hand. An expert witness could be a backwoods trapper with a third-grade education but unique knowledge of various kinds of traps, should that knowledge be relevant in a case.

Nonetheless, because technical training figures into expertise in mental health, establishing the mental health professional's credentials usually explores the individual's formal education, experience, degrees, professional practice, publications, memberships in professional organizations, experience in court and with similar cases, licenses, boards, and other certifications. Providing the attorney with a current *curriculum vitae* ahead of time guides the qualification process.

The qualification process is usually brief and painless, even under questioning by opposing counsel, as long as the witness has presented him or herself accurately and has the expertise to speak to the matters at hand. No attorney wants to discover that the so-called expert has never seen a similar case, has expertise far afield of that under litigation, or has misled others about his or her qualifications. Unfortunately, the mental health professions have suffered a number of imposters. We still hear now and then of someone professing to hold a doctorate in psychology whose doctorate is really in another field—or not a genuine degree at all. One alert attorney even subpoenaed a prospective expert witness's diploma to contradict his claims and discredit his testimony—evidence indeed that crime doesn't pay!

In some cases, opposing counsel will "stipulate," or accept, the witness's qualifications without a formal presentation to save time and get on with the testimony. Such cases are usually heard only by a judge and not a jury, and usually with a judge already familiar with the expert's background or willing to review a *vitae* to save time.

Expert Privileges—and Responsibilities

Testimony then proceeds with the witness responding to questions from retaining and opposing counsel as truthfully and as fully as the data examined allows. Expert witnesses differ from other witnesses in several ways. Unlike other witnesses, they may offer opinions in testimony and infer and conclude based on their expertise. They are not restricted to reporting factual or first-hand observations. However, their conduct in the courtroom should follow the conventions by which all witnesses abide. They should try to direct responses to the jury if there is one. If they can not answer questions in the forms in which they were asked, they should request restatements. If they do not understand questions, they should ask for clarification. If they do not know the answer to a question, their only appropriate response is, "I don't know."

If an attorney objects to another attorney's question, the witness should not answer or stop talking until the objection is overruled (denied) or sustained (upheld). Forgetting a question during the discussion of an objection happens frequently and is no cause for embarrassment; the witness should simply ask that it be repeated when the discussion ends.

Nonverbal communication plays a role in expert testimony as well (Stuffelbean, 1991). A "frozen" monotonic recital is less effective than responses with appropriate inflection and natural gesturing. Pauses can indicate thoughtful reflection, or, if they are too long, uncertainty, even deceit. Slow, firm speech can project an air of confidence while meek responses may damage credibility. In short, the principles of effective public speaking apply in the courtroom just as they do in other public settings.

In discussing the history of mental health testimony, we noted that expert witnesses can not simply support their opinions with their opinions; that is, they can not say "This is my opinion because I say it is." Rather, they must justify their conclusions and explain the bases for them. Thorough evaluations and well-considered conclusions—"doing the homework"—should make justification and explanation simple tasks.

Another rule of effective expert testimony is to understand the role of the expert witness. That role is not of advocate. Advocacy for one's opinions—conviction that they are sound—is acceptable, but it should be stated judiciously to avoid the appearance of advocacy for either attorney's cause. The expert witness should feel free to pause briefly while formulating a response rather than feeling pressure to blurt out an immediate reply. Such a pause suggests thoughtfulness, not indecisiveness, and it will help the expert respond clearly.

Another rule that results in clarity is so simple yet so often disregarded by many mental health experts. That rule is to speak in plain English. While many mental health professionals believe clinical jargon and technical terms lend precision to their own thinking and simplify communication with their colleagues, most judges and juries are not familiar with the language of mental health. Experts should avoid everything that smacks of "psychobabble" or risk being disregarded even when they later switch to cogent English.

Surviving Cross Examination

In general, direct examination, questioning by the attorney who retained the witness, is relatively straightforward and polite. Cross examination, questioning by opposing counsel, presents a somewhat different challenge. It is the job of opposing counsel to discredit expert testimony or at least reformulate it to be less damaging to the opposing counsel's client. Sometimes this process of impeachment attacks the credentials of the expert.

Cross-examining counsel may ask how much experience the expert has had in courtroom testimony and in dealing with cases similar to that being heard. Challenges to expertise take various forms, but one tactic often used against psychologists and social workers is to ask with a hint of disdain, "You are not a medical doctor, are you?" The questioner is attempting to put the expert on the defensive and to raise questions about his or her expertise in the minds of the jurors. The response? Neither defense nor apology is necessary; a polite "no" and an explanation of one's field of expertise usually disarm the challenger.

Another gambit used on cross examination is, "How much are you being paid for your testimony?" The attempt, of course, is to brand the expert as a hired gun whose testimony is for sale. A simple response that the expert is being paid for time and expertise, but that testimony *per se* is not for sale, usually ends the gambit. A less obvious variation is, "You are a professional expert witness, are you not?" The expert can address the innuendo by reflecting that he or she is a professional who sometimes also serves as an expert witness.

Sometimes, the cross-examining attorney asks, "Isn't your opinion (or psychology) subjective?" The attorney is implying that the expert is either not being objective or is basing conclusions on something akin to reading tea leaves, in either case, that the testimony does not meet the Frye (1923) criteria of basis in scientific principles or accepted standards of practice. The expert witness might explain the scientific bases of the field of psychology or the data on which an opinion rests. However, the witness should be careful when using the word "subjective"; its connotation in law is very different than in the behavioral sciences. "Subjective experience" may interest the clinician, but the legal system regards it with suspicion.

Another tactic used to reveal rigidity or lack of impartiality is to begin a question with, "Isn't it possible that . . . ?" Although answering "Of course it's possible—though not probable—that . . . " can lead the witness to support opposing opinion, experts must remember that testimony is based on reasonable medical or psychological certainty, not absolute fact. No one in the courtroom expects the witness to be infallible, but all hope that he or she recognizes his or her own fallibility. To answer a request for absolutes with absolutes, short of Benjamin Franklin's certainty about death and taxes, is pure folly.

Hypothetical questions present another interesting challenge. Here the attorney asks the expert to assume certain data as "facts" and draw conclusions from them. Hypothetical questions can help the expert address possibilities beyond those that the information at hand reflects. For example, one might be asked, "Doctor, would it change your opinion to assume that the defendant was treated for depression in 1985?" This question allows the expert to comment on the relevance of an earlier condition should he or she choose to do so.

But the data the expert is asked to assume may contain discordant or contradictory elements that lay a trap. Rather than a simple question like the one above, the expert might be asked "Doctor, if the day before the homicide the defendant had professed undying love for the victim, told a friend he was hearing voices coming from the radio, and said he felt married to the victim, what would you conclude?" Careful! Clarify each element rather than trying to respond to the entire set of conditions at once. What kind of voices were coming from the radio? Was the radio turned on? What connection did the voices have to the profession of love?

Hypothetical questions may include known facts, further data unknown to the expert, or erroneous information. Opposing counsel will probably object to the last, but hypothetical questions should be regarded with caution. If they inject confusion into the proceedings, the expert should say so.

Another question, most often put to the novice expert witness and usually delivered in a partly scolding tone, is "Have you discussed this case with anyone?" Counsel is implying a horrible breach of conduct to have done so, and in some circumstances that is appropriate, so the witness is tempted to blurt out, "No!" In almost every case, however, the witness has discussed the case with attorneys, investigators, and other professionals involved in it, which cross-examining counsel will quickly point out. The result is an embarrassed witness whose credibility is shot.

Some cross-examining attorneys hope witnesses neither listen nor remember carefully and refer to statements made under direct examination but with slight distortions. The expert must remember exactly what question was asked earlier and exactly the response to avoid getting caught. For example, the attorney might ask, "Doctor, on direct examination, you said that the defendant would panic if he heard a car backfire, isn't that correct?"

It's easy to not listen carefully and answer, "Yes." However, the cross-examiner could then cite a witnessed incident in which that did not occur, damaging the expert's testimony. Instead, the expert might respond, "No. What I said was that the defendant *might* panic if he heard a car backfire."

Other attorneys use a technique borrowed from direct sales, to establish a rhythmic and positive response set by asking a series of questions that require affirmative answers. The witness is then more likely to answer a final and incriminating question affirmatively. Consider the following dialogue:

Attorney: "Doctor, you said that the defendant was in an agitated state at the time, isn't that correct?"

Witness: "Yes."

Attorney: "Doctor, you said that the defendant was also angry at the time, isn't that correct?"

Witness: "Yes."

Attorney: "Doctor, you further said that the defendant was extremely frightened at the time, isn't that correct?"

Witness: "Yes."

Attorney: "In other words, Doctor, he was violently out of control, was he not?"

If he was not, the witness should not get caught up in the rhythm of the previous exchange but say so and, if asked, explain why.

There are many other gambits used on cross examination specific to the cases being heard. However, the effective witness can emerge with dignity and credibility if he or she listens thoughtfully, asks for clarification when necessary, takes his or her time to respond, and answers truthfully.

Maintaining Perspective

Just as the expert witness is not an advocate, he or she is not on trial. Expert testimony is only a portion of the evidence introduced in a case, and it is weighed in the context of the whole case. Expert witnesses do not win or lose; they simply aid the finders of fact as best they can. They should not personalize courtroom events in which other professionals are trying to do the best they can. Effective expert witnesses are always aware that they do not set forth conclusions of law and that their obligations are to be polite, clear, not defensive, and professional. When their testimony ends, they leave the courtroom, for they know that this is not their battle.

REFERENCES

Brodsky, S. L. "The Mental Health Professional on the Witness Stand: A Survival Guide." In Soles, B., ed., *Psychology in the Legal Process.* New York: Spectrum Publications, 1977, 269–276.

Brodsky, S. L. *Testifying in Court: Guidelines and Maxims for the Expert Witness.* Washington, DC: American Psychological Association, 1991.

Frye vs. U. S., 293 F. 1013 (DC Cir.), 1923.

Stufflebean, D. "The Expert Witness: Knowledge and Communication," *Journal of the Kansas Bar Association,* Vol. 60, No. 7.

Section V
OTHER CONSIDERATIONS

Chapter 19

QUALIFICATIONS OF THE FORENSIC PSYCHOLOGIST

The ethical guidelines for forensic psychologists (*Law and Human Behavior,* 1991) define forensic psychology as "all forms of professional psychological conduct when acting, with definable foreknowledge, as a psychological expert on explicitly psychologal issues, in direct assistance to courts, parties to legal proceedings, correctional and forensic mental health facilities, and administrative, judicial, and legislative agencies acting in adjunctive capacity." In the simplest terms, forensic psychology is the application of psychological practice, principles, and research within the legal system. It is the point at which psychology and law meet. The same is true for psychiatry.

A forensic psychologist, then, is one who regularly engages in the practice of forensic psychology as it is defined above. Many psychologists—and other mental health professionals—come into contact with the legal system by a variety of means, for example as therapists to parties involved in legal actions or resources to attorneys seeking information about psychological conditions. However, it is the mental health expert who "regularly" and with "foreknowledge" engages in such activities and who has specialized knowledge of psycholegal issues and practices who is the forensic specialist. And, in addition to serving as expert witnesses in court, forensic specialists may also serve as resources to other functions of the legal system—corrections or police selection and training, for instance.

The Ethics of Forensic Mental Health

To these ends, the forensic specialist has an ethical obligation both to maintain a reasonable understanding of the legal and professional standards governing the practice of forensic mental health and to adhere to those standards. Standards for psychologists are set forth in the Ethical Standards for Psychologists (APA, 1987) and supplemented by the Speciality Guidelines for Forensic Psychologists (*Law and Human Behavior,* 1991).

Principal among these standards are maintaining impartiality and confidentiality. The forensic psychologist must also ascertain that a party to legal proceedings is represented by counsel. Finally, the expert must be competent. The expert may not stray from those areas in which he or she truly has training, knowledge, and experience to have earned the status of "expert" nor to depart from "state of the art" practices. As Chapter 8 describes, predicting dangerousness with absolute certainty, for example, is clearly beyond current capabilities and would be a serious breach of professional practice. Let's examine each of these standards more closely.

Impartiality is absolutely imperative. The mental health expert must not "work for" anyone involved in a legal proceeding. So, agreeing to contingency fees—payments made only if the party calling the expert wins the case, and sometimes a percentage of the award—are unethical. Instead, mental health professionals should charge for their time at their standard rates for consultation. To avoid the potential influence of having moneys owed that might go unpaid in the event of unfavorable reports, many forensic specialists receive retainers when they begin work for the fees they expect to charge and then settle any difference at the end of the case.

Maintaining confidentiality is especially tricky, since by definition the expert witnesses divulges information imparted during sessions normally considered private. If the court orders an evaluation, then the court receives the findings, and privilege of communication does not apply. The mental health expert should explain to the client/patient that he or she will share information from the evaluation with others and obtain written release to do so. Attorney-client privilege can add another level of confidence to maintain. For example, an attorney requesting an evaluation of a client may not want that information divulged to others than him or herself.

When Responsibilities Collide

Not surprisingly, dilemmas can arise. Consider this example. Ordinarily, a therapist's records are protected by privilege. However, when a patient is involved in a lawsuit and records from therapy are relevant to the suit, privilege may be waived. Professional ethics permit the therapist to honor a subpoena whether records are relevant or not.

In one case, a therapist was seeing a patient who was involved in an accident that resulted in litigation. The suit involved no claim of emotional damage nor even allusion to one. Nevertheless, opposing counsel tried to subpoena the therapist's records. The subpoena was issued, and the patient became very upset.

As a compromise, the judge might have reviewed the records *in camera,* or privately in chambers, to decide their relevance to the pending litigation. Only those portions, if any, that had bearing on the case would be disclosed in court. However, the patient objected even to that. Two alternatives were left. In the first, the therapist would turn the records over and risk the loss of the therapeutic relationship. Or, the therapist could refuse to turn them over and risk being found in contempt of court.

The therapist found a third option and one which worked. He requested permission from the court to work through obtaining a release from the patient to the judge to review information for relevance to the case. In the end, he was able to comply with the terms of the subpoena and maintain the therapeutic relationship, but the process took time and creativity.

Additional Responsibilities

Forensic specialists should determine that subjects have legal counsel before proceeding with any evaluation. Sometimes people contemplating litigation seek psychological evaluations when it is not in their best legal interest to do so. Information obtained in evaluation is, as the example above shows, subject to discovery or subpoena, and mental health professionals risk contributing to people's legal undoings, however unwittingly. There are exceptions, of course; emergencies may call for treatment first and legal counsel second, while individuals acting *pro se,* or as their own attorneys, must decide for themselves whether psychological evaluations will help their cases.

The need for competence goes without saying. The situations discussed in this book demonstrate the critical nature of expert mental health testimony. Quite literally, it can influence decisions about life and death, not to mention decisions about competence to stand trial or to manage one's affairs, custody, and a host of other situations. Forensic specialists must ensure that their educations have provided adequate preparation and that they are up-to-date on matters of both psychology and law.

They should obtain licenses from the states in which they want to practice. Their curricula vitae should be current and correct.

Advanced Certification

State licensing agencies set minimum standards for competence. However, both psychology and psychiatry have mechanisms for recognizing advanced competence in forensics through board certification. The American Board of Professional Psychology awards its Diploma in Forensic Psychology to experts in the field. Psychiatry has analogous standards for board certification under the auspices of the American Academy of Psychiatry and Law. The certification process is currently under revision, however, and may be subsumed under the American Board of Psychiatry (Innes, 1992).

Those applying for the Diploma in Forensic Psychology must have earned doctorates in psychology, be licensed, be members in good standing of the American or Canadian Psychological Association or the American Psychology—Law Society, and have accumulated more than one thousand hours of actual forensic experience over at least five years of practice. Four of those years must follow receipt of the doctorate. Those with earned L.L.B. or J.D. degrees may substitute their legal training for two of the five years of practice in psychology, but they must still meet the requirement of one thousand hours of actual experience in forensic psychology. In addition, they must demonstrate at least one hundred hours of specialized training as forensic practitioners.

After the board verifies an applicant's credentials and experience, it requests two work samples demonstrating the applicant's knowledge and expertise in forensic matters. Within one year of the request, the applicant submits reports of two actual cases, with parties involved appropriately disguised, which the board reviews to determine that they reflect "a high degree of professional skill and maturity" (ABPP 1992).

After the board reviews and accepts the work samples, applicants are scheduled for final oral examinations. These three-hour examinations, conducted by panels of three diplomates in forensic psychology, have two parts. The first is a defense of the work samples showing an advanced level of competence and a professional manner. The second is more general and covers a range of issues in forensic psychology, including ethics, case law, and methods. Oral examinations are usually held within six months but must be held within a year of notification of eligibility.

The standards to which all forensic specialists adhere and the process of obtaining advanced certification are rigorous. However, they help ensure that mental health professionals involved in forensics bring the skills, knowledge, and levels of ethical and professional conduct they need to their assignments.

REFERENCES

American Board of Professional Psychology. *Information Concerning Board Certification in Forensic Psychology and the American Board of Forensic Psychology.* Columbia, Mo: American Board of Professional Psychology, 1992.

American Psychological Association. *Casebook on Ethical Principles of Psychologists.* Washington, DC: American Psychological Association, 1987.

"Committee on Ethical Guidelines for Forensic Psychologists," *Law and Human Behavior,* Vol. 15, No. 6, 1991.

Innes, R. Personal communication, May 16, 1992.

Chapter 20

EFFECTIVE COMMUNICATION BETWEEN THE MENTAL HEALTH PROFESSIONAL AND ATTORNEY

When a mental health professional is called on for an expert opinion, his or her first contact is usually with the attorney representing the client to be assessed. As Chapter 3 notes, the relationship between mental health professional and attorney begins between people whose frames of reference, language, and goals are different. Out of this relationship come, we hope, the best use of the expert and the most effective presentation of his or her testimony—outcomes that both meet the objectives of the expert and the attorney and serve the best interests of the client. Effective communication between the two helps to ensure those outcomes.

Before an Evaluation Begins

Before accepting a referral or beginning an evaluation, the mental health professional should take several steps. First, he or she should clarify the objectives of his or her assignment. Usually, the expert is retained in the hope that his or her testimony will support the attorney's case. However, supporting the attorney's case is not the expert's goal; the expert seeks to complete a thorough, professional evaluation. So, the expert should ensure that the attorney understands the expert's obligation and does not seek a "hired gun." Clarifying the issues and how one's expertise applies, while establishing an unambiguous role as an objective evaluator, is the first step. This step serves the attorney's needs too; neither the expert nor the attorney wants to get ambushed later because data were biased or reviewed in a biased way.

When specific legal criteria are involved, the expert should clarify with the attorney exactly what those criteria are, first in the language of the law and then of mental health. For example, what is the legal standard for insanity in the state where a case is being tried? Sometimes criteria for insanity are quite complex. What are the criteria for competence to testify? Custody? Next, which of the criteria applied in a case can a mental health professional address, and how? Often, because psychological variables are not the only considerations in a legal action, the mental health expert addresses only one aspect of the case. For example, the expert may investigate only personality make-up as it relates to the severity of a crime and the defendant's past record in certifying a juvenile to stand trial as an adult. Furthermore, the expert should limit his or her involvement to appropriate aspects and not inject opinions beyond those requested.

Clarifying one's role also clears up confusion that may result from the misuse of mental health terms. A court once referred a couple involved in a custody dispute for "counseling" when what the court wanted was a custody evaluation. The distinction between the two means far more to the mental health professional than the layperson, for the tasks are completely different, and clarifying the request avoids confusion. Communicating in plain English is the best course: "anxious," for example, may mean something different to the attorney than to the mental health professional, while "affect" as a noun meaning "emotion" is seldom heard outside the world of mental health.

Sometimes the mental health professional is asked to help in a case within his or her expertise but not given access to address the issues at hand. Chapter 12 describes the limitations on custody recommendations when the expert interviews only one parent. A similar situation occurs when a mental health professional is asked to evaluate an alleged child sexual abuser to validate or challenge the charges. Such a result can not occur. The expert can evaluate the alleged perpetrator and make statements about personality make-up, amenability to treatment, and prognosis. But without evaluating the entire situation, especially the child, context, other records of the event, even sometimes other family members, the mental health professional can usually not address the allegations in full. He or she should discuss such limits with the attorney as soon as they become apparent so that the attorney's expectations remain realistic.

The mental health professional should also discuss fees at the beginning of the case. As noted earlier, working on retainer is usually the wisest course, and the expert should estimate approximately how much time will be required. The attorney may explain the arrangement and estimate to the client, and the client, of course, should agree to it as well.

Early on, the mental health expert should request as much relevant information about the case—"good" and "bad"—as is available. Occasionally he or she will be denied it. In a child protection case, both the state and respondent parent retained mental health professionals to evaluate the parent. The case involved so much animosity that the attorneys finally agreed to a third, "independent" evaluation. That evaluation was to occur "from scratch," with no access for the new evaluator to earlier evaluations. The process was hardly an ideal one for the third expert to enter, but the mutual goal of "objectivity" justified it to the attorneys and clients involved.

The mental health professional and attorney should discuss the issue of privileged information. The situation in a forensic case is more complex than in a therapeutic relationship. While those involved in a forensic evaluation usually expect that the expert will discuss the subject and evaluation with the attorney, the wise expert obtains a written release to do so from the subject.

Attorney-client privilege protects information about the subject, but once the mental health professional is named as a potential testifying expert, the rules change. Everything in the professional's file is open to inspection or discovery by opposing counsel (Feder, 1991). However, the mental health professional must not remove information from the file; stiff penalties for doing so may apply, and the professional's credibility is certainly compromised.

When the Evaluation is Complete

After all of these issues are discussed and understood, the evaluation proceeds and the results are communicated to the attorney. Various events may follow. When written reports are submitted to attorneys for both sides, the results are known to both sides, as they should be. However, other cases may proceed differently. Consider a defense attorney's request for an evaluation of a client charged with first degree murder. The attorney hoped to find a basis for a plea of insanity or diminished capacity. Because the basis for such a plea is "mental disease or defect" except for criminal pathology as described by state statutes, and the mental health professional found no such disease or defect, the expert discussed his findings with the attorney and the story ended there; the expert did not even prepare a written report.

Preparing to Testify

If findings are to result in expert testimony, the expert will usually meet with the retaining attorney to review those findings, their strengths and weaknesses, and ways of presenting them most effectively in court. This stage often presents the greatest opportunity for conflict. The attorney seeks testimony to cast the most favorable light on the case. But the expert must ensure that testimony does not extend beyond that which can be supported by the data, science, and the expert's expertise. The expert's responsibility to stay within bounds serves the attorney's interests too; as the case of Barefoot vs. Estelle demonstrates, "absolute and one hundred percent" certainty does no one any good.

Sometimes the mental health professional's conclusions are important or interesting to him or her but not to the attorney. Finding that a defendant has a fascinating multiple personality may be exciting clinically, but if it does not address the legal issues at hand, the attorney will probably not use the information. The attorney is the choreographer and must take the lead in directing expert testimony.

The expert should point out weaknesses in the data or findings or results which may support the other side. Data which partially speak against the retaining attorney's position are not data to be buried; on the contrary, the attorney will most likely present them to the court during direct examination as evidence of that side's objectivity, fairness, and honesty and to mitigate the greater negative impact of its revelation on cross-examination.

Some attorneys prefer to rehearse witnesses' testimony. Rehearsals can help both sides prepare; they also point up differences between the attorney's hopes and the expert's opinions. However, both sides must be careful to remain flexible. A witness who only knows a script will appear lost and befuddled when events in the trial take a different tack. When that occurs, the expert should focus on the data, his or her interpretation of them, and the bases for that interpretation. The result should be an open, honest, and knowledgeable presentation.

Sometimes the expert's findings do not support the attorney's initial position but they may open up an alternative. Consider the situation of a man charged with first-degree murder. In the throes of an on-again, off-again divorce, he had made numerous threats to kill his wife if she left him, and eventually he did. After being charged, he was acting distressed but, according to his attorney, not in the way the attorney expected under the circumstances. The attorney raised the question of an insanity plea and requested an examination of his client under the ALI standard.

Evaluation of the defendant showed no mental disease or defect great enough to obliterate his ability to distinguish right from wrong or to make him unaware that his actions were wrong. Nor was there evidence to reflect an irresistible impulse in the homicide. The basis for an insanity plea, in the expert's opinion, simply did not exist.

However, in reviewing the psychological data and other records, what emerged was the probability that the defendant did not intend to kill his wife at the time that he did. He may have wanted to before, even intended to and suppressed the intent, but when he actually murdered her, he did so spontaneously, quickly, and impulsively, during an argument not about divorce but about going on a shopping trip together. The basis for a diminished capacity defense began to emerge, and the defendant was convicted of homicide in the second degree, not in the first.

This example shows the value of effective communication between mental health professionals and attorneys who work together. While the mental health professional should avoid using jargon, the attorney should be familiar both with mental health language and practice. Sometimes it is easy to dismiss the behavioral and social sciences as soft and bewildering, yet the professions of law and mental health are inextricably intertwined. Decisions about human motivation and mental state must be made, and to dismiss the behavioral sciences is to have to make those decisions with less objective and reliable data than the sciences can supply.

Effective Communication Throughout the Relationship

Communication between attorneys and mental health professionals is essential at the beginning, throughout, and at the conclusion of the cases on which they cooperate. Feder (1991) describes the milestones they pass together: the initial engagement, the investigation, the preliminary report, the final report, the legal process of discovery, and the actual trial. Effective collaboration, which requires listening carefully to one another and responding in terms the other understands, serves both disciplines and the best interests of the client at every critical point.

REFERENCE

Feder, H. *Succeeding as an Expert Witness.* New York: Van Nostrand, 1991.

INDEX

D

V

W

Z